Introduction

This book is intended to be helpful to all of those who are in the process of developing a volunteer program, or all of those who already have one which they would like to improve.

Essential Volunteer Management is one of a series of works about volunteer involvement produced by VMSystems. It is intended to provide a basic text on operating a volunteer program, and it is a companion to 'idea' books such as *101 Ideas for Volunteer Programs*, 'sample' books such as *Volunteer Management Forms* and more in-depth treatments such as *Developing Your Leadership Potential*.

We would like to thank the thousands of participants in workshops who shared with us both their problems and their solutions. You are too numerous to mention and too important to forget.

Table of Contents

Essential Volunteer Management

Authors:
Steve McCurley
and
Rick Lynch

Designer:
Denise A. Vesuvio

The Volunteer Management Series of VMSystems

Design and graphics by Denise A. Vesuvio,
VMSystems, Washington, DC

ISBN 0-911029-14-1

The Volunteer Management Series is a product of
VMSystems and Heritage Arts Publishing,
Downers Grove, IL

(708) 964-1194

Chapter One

An Introduction to Volunteer Management

Volunteering

Volunteering has long been a pervasive tradition in American history. Since the days of de Tocqueville, commentators have noted the American penchant for forming voluntary groups of citizens to work on common problems and interests.

Currently, volunteering is one of the most commonplace activities in society. During the 1980's the level of volunteering has stayed at between 45-50% of the adult population. In a survey conducted by the Gallup Poll organization in 1987 over 80 million adults reported volunteering during the year, contributing a total of 19.5 billion hours.

Volunteer-Utilizing Agencies

The recipients of this donation of volunteer time are equally varied. The majority of volunteers work with non-profit agencies or causes, but in 1985 over 18% of those who volunteered did so for government agencies and almost 7% volunteered for a for-profit institutions, such as a nursing homes or hospitals.

The importance of volunteers to these agencies can scarcely be overstated. For non-profit organizations, volunteers can often make the difference between remaining in operation or being forced to close. In some ways volunteers are as important to charitable causes as are donations of money. In 1987 the estimated value of volunteer time given to non-profit organizations was about $120 billion; the value of cash contributions was of almost equal value. Without the support of either of these types of donations from the public, most non-profit organizations would be unable to operate.

Volunteers

Volunteers come in all shapes, ages, and sizes. With almost half of the population engaged in volunteering, it should not be surprising that the 'typical' volunteer can actually be almost anyone. Volunteering stretches across all age categories, with the largest amount of volunteering being done by those between ages 30-45, but with almost a quarter of those either under age 20 or over age 65 being involved in volunteer work.

Volunteering is equally represented among genders, with almost exactly half of both the male and female population involved. Volunteering is also little affected by racial distinctions.

Reasons to Volunteer

Volunteers get involved for a variety of reasons. Among those most often cited are:

"Wanted to help others"

"Felt obligated to give back what I got"

"Sense of citizenship"

"Religious feelings"

"Interested in the work to be done"

"Desire for involvement with a group of friends"

A typical volunteer will experience a variety of motivations, ranging from the altruistic to the self-interested, throughout their volunteering 'career', and, indeed, may have that motivation vary considerably as they work over time with a single organization.

The patterns of a volunteer's connection with an agency or cause will also vary. Overall, the average volunteer donates about 4.7 hours per week to his or her volunteer work, usually spreading this time out over 2-3 organizations. Some volunteers, however, are dedicated to or involved with only a single cause, and often spend hundreds of hours a year working on that effort.

Volunteers also vary in the length of time they stay with an organization. Some volunteers prefer to work with many organizations, changing from group to group within the course of a single year. Others are committed to a specific organization or cause, remaining with that group for decades.

Changing Styles of Volunteer Involvement

Volunteering now appears to be going through some changes related to the 'style' in which people choose to participate. In some ways we seem to be moving toward a system in which there are two distinct types of volunteers.

One type might be called the *"Long Term Volunteer"*.

The Long Term Volunteer

The Long Term Volunteer matches the traditional notion of the volunteer who is dedicated to a cause. Among the characteristics of the Long Term Volunteer are the following:

- Dedication to a cause or to an organization. The Long Term Volunteer has a strong sense of affiliation with the volunteer effort and is connected in an 'institutional' sense, i.e. considers him/herself an "owner" of the effort.
- The Long Term volunteer is commonly recruited either by 'self-recruitment' (finding the agency because of an already existing personal commitment to the cause) or by growth from within the system.
- The Long Term Volunteer will tend to shape their own job and the duration of their work, adapting their time and energies to whatever is necessary to make the cause succeed. Long Term Volunteers tend to be 'generalists.'
- Motivation for the Long Term Volunteer is a matter of both "Achievement" and "Affiliation", and often recognition is best expressed as a greater opportunity for involvement or advancement in the cause.
- The key to working with a Long Term Volunteer is to "Think With" them, acting as though they were partners in an effort.

Many established organizations have relied for years on Long Term Volunteers, designing jobs that require a steady donation of time over a prolonged period.

○ ▼ ❑ ○ ▼ ❑ ○ ▼ ❑ ○ ▼ ❑ ○

The Short Term Volunteer

During the past ten years, however, a different style of volunteering has begun to develop. For purposes of comparison, this style might be called that of the "*Short Term Volunteer*". Among the characteristics of the Short Term Volunteer are:

- A general interest in an organization or cause, but usually not of extreme depth. The Short Term Volunteer is not a 'believer' or a 'joiner'.
- The Short Term Volunteer is commonly recruited through one of three methods. They may connect with an organization because of a particular volunteer job in which they are interested, and it is the type of work that attracts them, not what the organization will try to accomplish through that work. They may be recruited through participation in a specific event, such as a weekend sports program or race. It will usually be the type of event that attracts them, and not necessarily the organization from whom the event is being conducted. Or they may be recruited by "forced choice", being 'asked' by a friend or employer to volunteer. Commonly they are volunteering for and because of their connection with the requestor, not from any knowledge of or commitment to the agency or cause.
- The Short Term Volunteer wants a well-defined job of limited duration. Many Short Term Volunteers can be considered 'specialists'. Usually the more limited the timeframe and the better delineated the scope of the required work, the easier it will be to recruit the Short Term Volunteer. A Short Term Volunteer may well volunteer throughout their lifetime, but they will tend not to remain too long with any single organization, or they will only work on jobs which allow them to closely control the extent of time which they donate to any organization.
- Motivation for the Short Term Volunteer is a matter of recognizing their personal achievement, not of recognizing their status within the group. Recognition is a matter of acknowledging their contribution.
- The key to working with a Short Term Volunteer is to "Think For" them, making sure that the time which they donate is well-utilized and not wasted on extraneous requirements.

Oddly enough, an individual may be a Short Term Volunteer with one group and a Long Term Volunteer with another group.

On balance, it seems that there is a clear shift occurring toward a preference for being a Short Term Volunteer. In attempting to cope with competing demands from work, home life, and the possibilities of involvement, potential volunteers are choosing to limit their participation by changing the way in which they allow themselves to become involved.

Implications

The impact of this changing style on volunteer management has been in several areas:

1. It has necessitated some major changes in job design and recruitment techniques. Agencies have been forced to make jobs 'smaller' and more manageable and to cater more to the requirements of the volunteer related to availability and duration.
2. Some agencies have encountered difficulties when Long Term Volunteers and Short Term Volunteers have worked together. The Long Term Volunteer may well view the Short Term as 'uncaring' or not committed to the agency. The lack of willingness of the Short Termer to devote the time and energy given by the Long Termer can be viewed with hostility.
3. To recruit Long Term Volunteers, who are actually both more desirable, easier to manage, and highly necessary to some leadership volunteer functions, agencies are having to rely more on 'promotion from within', grooming volunteers to assume more responsibilities and slowly convincing them to commit to greater donation of time.
4. Agencies are facing greater competition for available Short and Long Term Volunteers. Increasingly, the volunteer is in a favorable bargaining position, sought by several agencies, and able to pick among those agencies for the position which best meets the needs and interests of the volunteer.

Volunteer Management

Volunteer programs also vary in style of operation. One might picture a continuum of programs ranging from those that are very structured, with a high degree of permanent staff supervision of volunteers (such as a volunteer program to aid those within a prison), to those that are primarily operated by volunteers themselves (such as a community crime watch program).

While the principles of volunteer management remain the same in both styles of program, the exact methods used will vary from the more institutional orientation to the more personal orientation.

The Volunteer Management Process

The process of volunteer management involves the following operations:

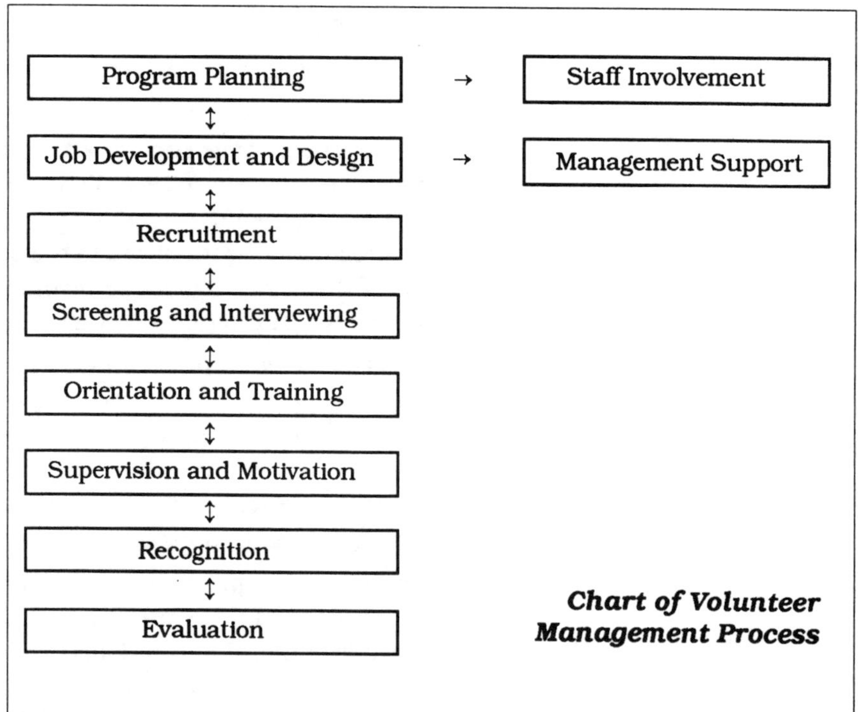

Chart of Volunteer Management Process

At any given moment, the normal volunteer program will be engaged, to one degree or another, in all of these processes.

The Geometry of Volunteer Involvement

Another way of looking at the process of volunteer management can be represented through the use of simple geometric figures. Throughout this book we will be referring to these figures as a way of representing what ought actually to be happening throughout the process of managing a volunteer program. We will be working with three simple shapes:

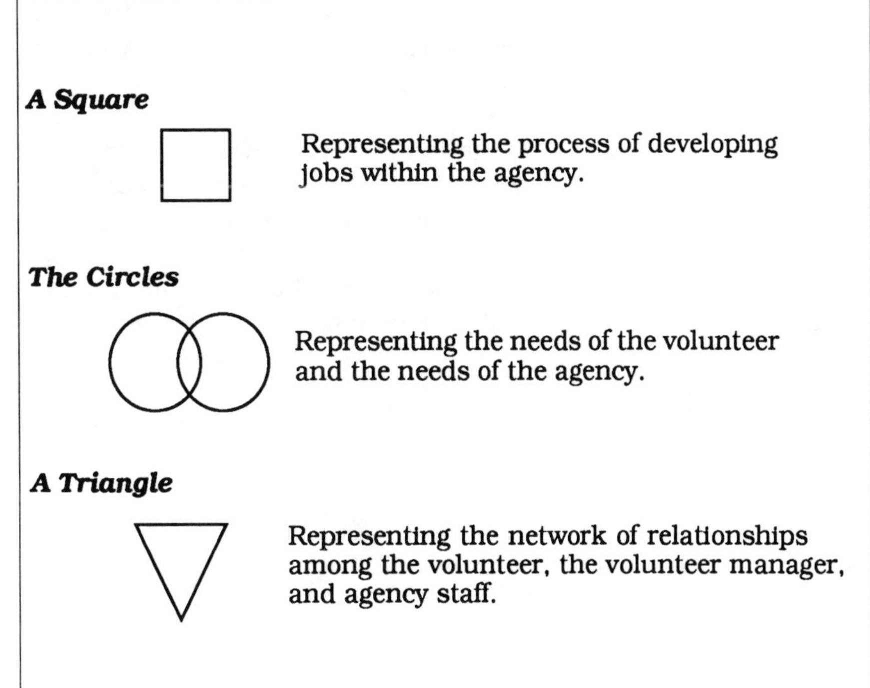

A Square
Representing the process of developing jobs within the agency.
The Circles
Representing the needs of the volunteer and the needs of the agency.
A Triangle
Representing the network of relationships among the volunteer, the volunteer manager, and agency staff.

Taken together, these three shapes illustrate the major tasks which must be accomplished in order for volunteer management to be effective.

○ ▼ ❑ ○ ▼ ❑ ○ ▼ ❑ ○ ▼ ❑ ○

Role of the Volunteer Manager

The key to this process is the volunteer manager. Volunteer programs do not work spontaneously, but require someone to devote the care and attention required for fitting together a complex system matching the needs of the agency with the needs of the community.

The best analogy for an effective volunteer manager is that of a consultant - the role requires working with other staff in the agency to analyze what needs to be, what can be done by part-time volunteer workers, and what will be attractive enough to motivate those volunteers. As a consultant, the volunteer manager must focus on meeting the needs both of staff and of volunteers.

Performing this role effectively requires the ability to relate well with people and to understand both their needs and wants; the ability to be flexible and adapt to changing demands and interests; and the ability to be creatively opportunistic, to identify a potential opportunity and create the structure which is necessary to make that opportunity happen.

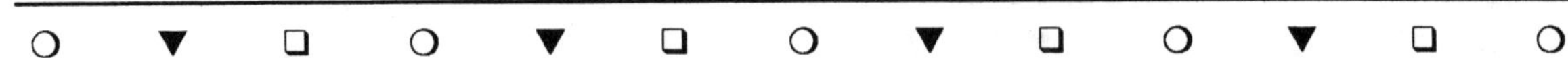

Chapter Two

Planning for a Volunteer Program

Getting Things Started

Some volunteer efforts have suffered from the problems generated by "spontaneous creation." This phenomenon occurs when an over-enthusiastic administrator learns of the potential of volunteer involvement and pronounces at a staff meeting: "*Let there be volunteers.*"

The assumption behind this pronouncement is that instituting a volunteer effort is simple and can be done instantaneously. The pronouncement is usually followed by the designation of some unsuspecting staff person as "in charge of volunteers", with the immediate assignment of "going out and rounding up a bunch of them."

Alas, effective volunteer management is simple in theory, but subtle in operation. It has all of the complexities of basic personnel management: job development, supervision, evaluation systems, etc. And it also has complexities all of its own. An interesting example, not seen as often in the environment of paid staff, is that of the over-enthusiastic worker. Quite often, a volunteer manager will have to deal with a volunteer who causes difficulties for the program not from a lack of motivation, but from a surplus of it. This volunteer will be so dedicated to the cause that they will expect and work for instant solutions to any problem that arises, and will not understand why the system sometimes operates so slowly. The volunteer will become impatient and infuriated with anyone, paid staff or volunteer, who doesn't give total dedication to making the system work perfectly, immediately.

Effective volunteer programs do not happen spontaneously, and they do not happen by accident. A well-designed program needs to consider many factors, and make many decisions before any volunteers are sought for the program.

Fitting Together the Puzzle

In a way, one might think about volunteer involvement with an agency as the construction of a puzzle.

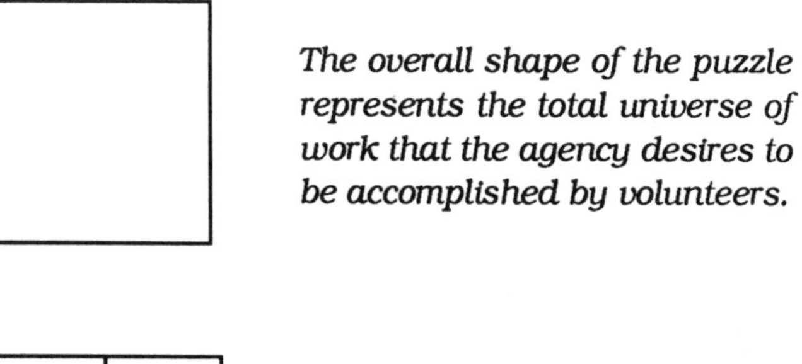

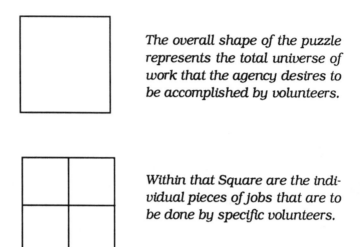

The overall shape of the puzzle represents the total universe of work that the agency desires to be accomplished by volunteers.

Within that Square are the individual pieces of jobs that are to be done by specific volunteers.

During the past ten years, the configurations of this puzzle have become increasingly complicated. The size of the square has increased, as agencies have developed broader needs for volunteers, involving volunteers in tasks previously reserved for paid staff. And the complexity of the job mix has changed, as agencies have had to develop more jobs designed for the short-term volunteer, jobs which requires a lesser time commitment and greater flexibility to meet the needs and interest of the short-term volunteer.

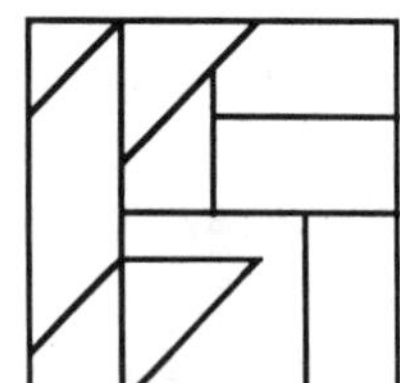

For the typical agency today, the puzzle more closely resembles a jigsaw puzzle, one that changes shapes every week.

The volunteer manager is responsible both for designing the overall puzzle shape and for fitting together the individual pieces that complete the puzzle. This has to be done in concert with both staff, who help design the parameters, and volunteers, who help determine the design of individual jobs.

Rationale for a Volunteer Program

The first step in constructing the design of an agency's volunteer program requires determining *why* the agency wishes to involve volunteers. This decision will influence the following:

- It will determine the types of jobs and responsibilities that the agency will create for volunteers.
- It will enable the agency to better explain to volunteers how and why they are contributing to the work of the agency.
- It will enable the agency to better explain to staff why volunteers are being sought.
- It will enable the agency to develop a plan for evaluating whether the utilization of volunteers has been effective.

Potential Rationales

There are many potential rationales for involving volunteers. These include:

1. Providing for community outreach or input.
2. Supplementing staff resources and experiences.
3. Gaining additional expertise.
4. Giving a more personal touch in services to clients.
5. Assisting in fundraising efforts.
6. Cost savings.

Reaching Agreement

It is highly desirable that some agreement is reached on this rationale. In a sense the rationale will represent part of the "mission" of the volunteer program. It will provide a quick and clear understanding of what benefit the agency thinks will be derived from utilization of volunteers, and provide a sense of purpose for the volunteer program. In essence, it should answer "*why are we doing this?*"

Staff Involvement

Throughout this process it is essential to involve all levels of staff. If volunteers are going to be working in conjunction with paid staff, whether for them or in support of them, it is essential that staff are in agreement about the purpose and worth of the volunteer program.

Staff who do not want to work with volunteers can destroy a volunteer effort, either through direct opposition or through indifference. If staff are not willing to cooperate in developing realistic jobs for volunteers, if they ignore volunteers or give them second class status in the agency, if they indicate by word or by action that volunteers are a hindrance not a help, then volunteers will quickly become disillusioned and de-motivated, and they will quickly find other agencies with which to volunteer.

Surveying Staff Attitudes

One method for assessing staff attitudes is to conduct a survey. The survey, which can be done either through interviewing or through a paper instrument, should ascertain:

1. *The level of experience of staff in working with volunteers:*

   Have they ever supervised volunteers before? Have they ever worked in an agency which utilized volunteers?

2. *Their level of comfort about utilizing volunteers:*

   Are there jobs which they feel volunteers should do, or should not do? Are there program elements, such as additional training for staff, that should be instituted?

3. *Any fears that staff may have about volunteer utilization:*

   Are there potential difficulties, such as legal liability questions, that should be addressed? Are there worries about loss of staff jobs by replacement?

The responses to this survey should tell the volunteer manager how staff are likely to react to the inclusion of volunteers, a topic which is covered later in the chapter on "Volunteer-Staff Relationships."

○ ▼ ❑ ○ ▼ ❑ ○ ▼ ❑ ○ ▼ ❑ ○

Top Management Support

It is also desirable to have the support of the top management of the agency. This support might be represented by the official adoption by the board of the agency of a policy supporting the use of volunteers, or by a position statement on volunteers approved by the chief staff of the agency.

It is important to note, however, that while it is desirable to have top management support for utilization of volunteers, it is not desirable to have that support become coercive in nature. It is not possible for management to *compel* staff to utilize volunteers. Opposing staff can too easily drive volunteers away or can too easily make it impossible for volunteers to be successful. What is desirable is an attitude of top management that encourages and rewards effective utilization by staff of volunteer resources, an approach using the 'carrot' not the 'stick'.

Organizational Climate

Overall organizational climate will also influence how volunteers can be utilized.

Volunteers will quickly become aware of overall agency attitudes, whether about how well the agency is doing, how things are done, or who and what is important to the agency. These sometimes subtle cues regarding agency style will influence the determination by volunteers of whether the agency is worth the donation of their time. Since the agency will become a work site for the volunteers, they are more likely to appreciate and stay at an agency which has a positive environment. What is needed is a sense of common mission and purpose, and an understanding that productive steps are being taken toward accomplishment of that mission and purpose.

Some indicators of a good organizational climate include:

- Clear sense of individual roles, with respect for roles of others
- Willingness to sacrifice for a goal
- Trust
- Tolerance and acceptance
- Open and honest communication
- Group identity: 'we're in this together'
- Inclusion, not exclusion

An organizational climate which is favorable toward volunteers will communicate two feelings or attitudes to the volunteers:

Acceptance:

That volunteers are welcomed by and connected with the overall purpose and operations of the agency.

Appreciation:

That each volunteer has a unique, recognized contribution to make to the purpose and operations of the agency.

Policies and Procedures

Volunteer program management also requires the creation of some formal rules and procedures. After determination of why volunteers are to be utilized, the agency will need to develop its own set of polices and procedures governing the utilization of volunteers. Policies should be developed in the following areas:

1. Attendance and absenteeism.
2. Performance review procedures.
3. Benefits: insurance, parking, continuing education.
4. Grievance procedures.
5. Reimbursement policies.
6. Use of agency equipment.and facilities.
7. Confidentiality requirements.
8. Probationary acceptance period.
9. Suspension and Termination.
10. Record-keeping requirements.

The policies will allow the volunteer manager to develop a consistent pattern of volunteer utilization, and will provide assistance in dealing with problem situations. Both the policies, and the procedures by which they will be implemented, should be developed in conjunction with staff, particularly if the agency is utilizing volunteers in a variety of different types of projects or activities.

If you have a question about the content of a policy or procedure, refer to the agency policies and procedures for paid staff. The rules should be as similar as possible: "when in doubt, copy."

Systems

The volunteer program will also need to develop some basic personnel-related systems. Volunteer programs operate with the essential forms required for any operation involving people: intake forms, job descriptions, evaluation instruments, etc. Individual records need to be maintained for each volunteer, giving their biographical and contact information, records of their positions and training, dates of connection with the agency, etc. The systems and files developed should match those of paid staff, and can often be the same forms.

Investigate the utilization of computer software packages to assist in these personnel functions. Software packages are now available (or can be custom-developed for your program) that will greatly aid you in keeping track of the names, skills, interests, and availability of your volunteers. They can greatly assist you in performing the paperwork functions of volunteer management, conserving your time to deal with those parts of the job which require human contact.

Systems should also address issues of legal liability and insurance. A risk management process should be undertaken to determine the extent of exposure to injury or legal action of both the volunteers and the agency. It should also help determine what actions the agency might take to lessen potential difficulties, such as instituting a confidentiality agreement with volunteers to protect the privacy of clients.

If it is determined that volunteers are exposed to suit or to personal injury then the agency should determine whether it can provide appropriate insurance coverage or can recommend to the volunteers that they ensure that they are protected by their individual insurance policies.

Evaluation

The plan for the volunteer program should also consider the process for evaluation of the volunteer program. The design of the program operations should include the management information systems which will enable staff, management, volunteers and the volunteer manager to determine how things are going on a regular basis.

The intent of evaluation is both to uncover problems (low rates of volunteer retention; need for additional training) and to reward accomplishment. Much like individuals, agencies and programs need to know when they are successful; without measurements of what success is and when is has been accomplished, it is impossible to know when you have 'won.'

In developing the evaluation plan, consider the following questions:

1. *What would volunteers like to know about themselves, about the program?*

   Hours contributed, benefit to program, etc.

2. *What would staff who work with volunteers like to know?*

   Numbers of volunteers in their department, impact of volunteers on clientele, etc.

3. *What would management like to know?*

   Who is utilizing volunteers, value of the volunteer time contributed to the agency, etc.

4. *What would you like to know?*

   What volunteers are coming from and what attracts them to the agency, rate of volunteer turnover, etc

Assessing Your Plan

Assess your plan for volunteer involvement by reviewing the following checklist. If you have not completed the items on the list, then you still have preparations to finish before you and your agency can effectively involve volunteers:

- ✓ Have we consulted with staff who will be working with this volunteer?
- ✓ Are these staff clear on what their role will be in working with the volunteer?
- ✓ Is a complete and accurate job description written for this position?

✓ Does the position description clearly identify the qualifications for the job and outline both the purpose and nature of the work to be done?

✓ Have we identified a working environment for the volunteer, in terms of supervisory relationships, work space, etc?

✓ Do we have a plan for seeking qualified applicants for the positions?

✓ Do we know how we will distinguish qualified applicants from unqualified applicants? Do we know what we will do with unqualified applicants?

✓ Do we have a plan for orienting and training this volunteer?

Closing

Resist the impulse to quickly initiate a volunteer effort. The time spent in planning and preparation will greatly reduce both confusion and problems that will arise later. Operate by these rules:

- Think first, and get the volunteers later. They'll appreciate your consideration.

- Do it right the first time, it's easier than having to do it over again.

Chapter Three

Creating Volunteer Jobs

Staff Involvement

The process of creating volunteer jobs begins with involving staff in developing ideas for work that can appropriately be done with volunteers. This process is one of the most important functions of the volunteer manager: without "good" jobs, the agency will have nothing of value to offer to volunteers. An agency which has interesting and productive jobs to offer will have an easy time attracting volunteers. An agency with boring or unsatisfying jobs will have an impossible time retaining volunteers.

Consulting with Staff

The most effective method of developing good jobs is to 'consult' with staff. During this process, the volunteer manager interviews staff to determine how they might best make use of volunteers. This interview does not consist of merely asking staff what jobs they might have for a volunteer, since this question is not likely to produce a creative response from staff who have no previous experience with volunteers.

Instead, the staff should be taken through a process first developed by Ivan Scheier, in which staff are asked their responses to the following questions:

1. *"What are the parts of your job that you really like to do?"*

   Responses might include working directly with clients, doing research, etc.

2. *"What are the parts of your job that you really dislike?"*

   Responses might include answering information requests, making presentations, etc.

3. *"What other activities or projects have you always wanted to do but never had the time for?"*

   Responses might include working with a new client group or starting a program in a new community.

The pattern of responses to these questions can then be used to put together a volunteer job that will be productive for both staff and volunteers. By focusing on the types of work that the staff does not want or has not had the time to do yet, a job can be developed which is both 'real' (i.e., it really needs to be done) and will be appreciated by the staff, who will have a vested interest in keeping the volunteer (otherwise they must go back to doing the work themselves or to forfeiting the new effort). Incentive is also offered to staff, in that they can concentrate more on doing things that they really want to do. The end result is that everyone is made happier.

The interview process can also be utilized to educate staff as to the correct 'shape' for a volunteer job request: timeframe, need for training, supervisory requirements, etc. Conducting the interview and jointly helping the staff develop the description of work to be done will greatly lessen the prospect of being bombarded with requests for impossible volunteers: "Someone to come in from 9-5, Monday through Friday, and do my filing."

Consulting Tools

To assist in this effort, it is helpful to have a number of tools, which can be utilized in showing staff what will be possible. These tools can be utilized in a "Menu" approach, giving staff lists of possibilities. The tools include:

1. A list of the types of jobs/functions that volunteers are already performing in the agency.
2. A list of types of job/functions that volunteers might be performing, based on work being done in other agencies in the community, or in similar programs across the country.
3. Skills/descriptions of already available volunteers.

These listings will serve to provide ideas on potential jobs to staff who do not have a clear understanding of the potential uses of volunteers within the agency. They will serve to broaden the perspective and improve the creativity of staff in developing interesting and challenging volunteer positions.

The Circle of Staff Needs

This process of staff involvement should be a continuous one. The volunteer manager should develop a process for on-going communication with staff, either by periodic follow-up interviews or through written communication, in which the process of new job development continues. One method for accomplishing this is to institute a "Work Wanted" section in the agency newsletter or via memo, in which volunteers jobs are highlighted or in which the skills or new volunteers are announced. The aim of this communication is to create a demand for additional types of volunteer effort.

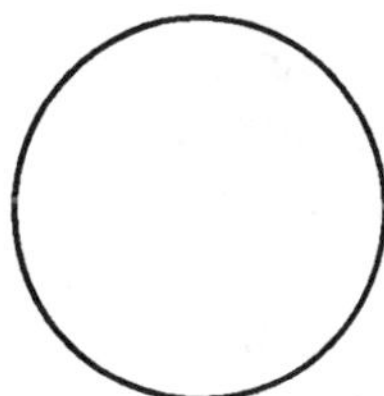

In essence what is being created through this process is the Circle of Staff Needs.

The Circle represents the needs and interests of the staff, formatted into a request for particular work to be done. The Circle includes a request for specific skills, time commitment, attitudes, etc, that in composite represent what the agency is looking for in a volunteer.

Designing Volunteer Jobs for Results

Volunteer jobs can be boring and unsatisfying, leading to burnout and turnover, or they can be interesting, challenging, and rewarding, leading to high enthusiasm and good results for the volunteer. The difference between the two depends in part on the person doing the job, since different people have different motivational needs and will find different jobs to be interesting or boring. It will also depend upon the design of the job itself.

Volunteer jobs are successful when volunteers are working in jobs they look forward to and want to do. If we fail to give volunteers such a job, we will be plagued by turnover, unreliability, and low morale, because a job people want to do is the cornerstone of all successful volunteer programs. While paid people will do a job that is unrewarding because they are paid for doing so, volunteers will not for long. This has given volunteers in general a reputation among some paid staff for being unreliable. To the contrary, if the volunteer does not find the job to be personally satisfying, the volunteer can be relied upon to quit and to seek another volunteer position.

The job descriptions of volunteers in most agencies look exactly like those of paid staff. The jobs tend to be designed around standard management practices of the non-volunteer world. Instead, when we design jobs for volunteers, we might more productively follow the principles of those who design games.

Games are voluntary activities that are designed to be intrinsically motivating. Games are so motivating, in fact, that people will spend lots of their time and money on expensive equipment and lessons in order to get better at them, a thing which is rarely true of work. Games are so well designed, in fact, that people will spend money just to get to see other people play them. If this were true of work, we wouldn't have to worry about funding; we could just sell tickets to those who wanted to watch us do the work.

The point is not that volunteering should be a game, but that it should have the same motivational qualities that games do, to such an extent that the volunteer truly *enjoys* and *benefits from* volunteering. In designing volunteer jobs, one should strive to include the following four elements that are present in games but rarely, alas, present in work:

Turf

The first factor is "turf." By turf, we mean that the volunteer has a sense of ownership, something they can point to and say "This is mine." This might be a particular product or event or geographic area. In the non-profit world, the turf is most often a volunteer's own client or project. There are many examples of volunteers having such responsibility: Big Brothers, phone workers in a crisis clinic, senior companions, and Foster Grandparents are all volunteers who have one or more clients who are 'theirs.'

One way of thinking about turf is that it gives the volunteer something to be in charge of and hence to be proud of. One way of meeting this is to give volunteers a project of their own that they can control, or an activity for which they have discrete responsibility.

Turf is destroyed when volunteers do only one of many activities which the agency conducts in providing a particular service to a particular person or group. In some social service agencies, for example, volunteers might do intake on clients, then hand the resulting paperwork over to someone else to determine the eligibility for services. When volunteers merely do one activity in a string of activities that finally end up in the client being served, they lose the intense satisfaction of helping others that drives most volunteer efforts. Although they know that somewhere down the line clients are being served, their sense of pride in this is diluted by all the others who have had a hand in that service. Similarly, volunteers fixing up a school will tend to get more satisfaction if they do all the activities related to fixing up particular room than if they do one activity (such as painting) in all the rooms. The first circumstance provides them with a sense of turf ("This is my room.") that the second circumstance does not. Because their sense of pride in the work is diluted and lost, such volunteers tend to burn out much faster than those who have full responsibility for a client or a project.

This is not to say that teamwork should be avoided in job design. Teams of people can also have turf. In one city, for example, there is an all-volunteer program which was formed when the parks department reduced maintenance personnel during a budget cut. Teams of volunteers had parks of their own which they kept free of trash and graffiti. In this case, the sense of ownership was met because the team could look at 'our park' and take pride in its appearance.

The Authority to Think

The difference between a team and a collection of isolated individuals who lack ownership is that a team has the authority to plan and evaluate its work and agree on who is going to do what. This authority to think is the second key element in good job design, whether for individuals or groups. With this authority the individual or group not only does the work but plays some part in deciding how to do it.

Many volunteer managers have a built-in resistance to allowing volunteers this authority. For one thing, the volunteer may only work a few hours per month and may have difficulty keeping up with what is going on. For another, standard management practice holds that it is the supervisor's job to do the planning and deciding and the employee's job to carry-out whatever the supervisor thinks should be done.

Indeed, when a volunteer first comes on board, this may be the most comfortable way to proceed. As volunteers learn the job and figure out what it going on, however, the fact that they are only doing what someone else decides begins to sap their motivation and dilute their feelings of pride in what they accomplish. They will tend either to resent being told what to do or to lose interest in the job. Either of these will increase the likelihood of the volunteers dropping out.

This does not mean that we should abdicate our responsibility for insuring good results from volunteers. Obviously, we can't afford to have all our volunteers doing whatever they think is best, without any guidance. We need to make sure that we are all working toward the achievement of a coordinated set of goals. What we can do, however, is involve them in the planning and deciding process so that they do feel a sense of shared authority over the 'how' of their job.

The process of managing all of this is explained further in the chapter on "Empowering Volunteers." For now, suffice it to say that in designing the job we should ask "How would a person who tells the volunteer what to do know what to tell him"? Or we could ask, "What does the volunteer's supervisory do in order to figure out what to tell the volunteer to do"? We can then include those thinking and planning tasks in the volunteer's job description, healing the schism between thinking and doing.

Responsibility for Results

The third critical element in developing a work structure that encourages excellence is to make sure that the volunteers are held responsible for achieving results rather than only performing a set of activities or 'job duties'. If volunteers are responsible for results or outcomes, they are focused on the end product of what they do, and they get the satisfaction of making progress toward a meaningful accomplishment. If, on the other hand, they are responsible only for the activities that may lead to some result, they are divorced from that satisfaction. A crime prevention volunteer for a police department, for example, will get a lot more satisfaction if they are responsible for reducing burglaries than if they see the job as the activity of knocking on doors to talk to people about planting 'hostile shrubbery' under their windows.

Most job descriptions for volunteers or for paid staff are not defined in terms of results. Instead, they merely list a series of activities that volunteer is supposed to perform. The result is never mentioned. Most often, in fact, the responsibility for the result is fragmented, with several people all having a few activities to perform if the result is to be achieved. In fact, the responsibility is often so fragmented that the volunteer loses sight of the result. As a direct consequence of this, results are poorly and inefficiently obtained and the volunteer get bored.

Questions to ask yourself in giving responsibility for results include, "What do I want to happen because of the work the volunteer is doing?" and "What kind of change do I want to occur?"

Keeping Score

The forth critical element in good job design is to decide how to measure whether the results are being achieved. If we don't do this, the statement of result will fail to have any motivating value, and it will be impossible for both volunteer and supervisor to know how well the volunteer is doing.

Many volunteer managers shy away from measuring volunteer performance, thinking that doing so would discourage or demotivate them. The opposite is more likely to be the case, however. If people can't tell how well they are doing, if they can't tell if they are succeeding or failing, they tend to get bored with the activity. There is also no incentive to try a different course of action if you don't know that your present course is failing.

For some jobs the measure of performance is fairly obvious and easy to state. In the case of the crime prevention volunteer working with a police department, for example, the number of burglaries in the area is a readily available statistic. By giving the challenge of reducing the total number of burglaries, we give the possibility of having a score to judge performance. Every time a burglary occurs in the area, the volunteer will naturally ask "What could have been done to prevent that?" These thoughts will spur creativity and effort, and encourage new and more effective approaches. If the job is defined instead as "engraving social security numbers of people's stereos", there is no feedback on how well the volunteer is doing, and there is little likelihood that more effective approaches will be tried.

In other cases, measurement may be more difficult. In the case of the Girl Scout leader whose result is to have girls develop self-assurance, we need to do some hard work to determine how we should measure progress. We might ask such questions as:

"How will be know if girls have more self-assurance?"

"What will we see if they are or aren't self-assured?"

"What questions could we ask them to determine their degree of self-confidence?"

Many volunteer managers don't want to do this much work and so take the easy course of holding the volunteer accountable only for performing a group of activities. By doing so, however, they deprive the volunteer of the ability to tell how they are doing and of any sense of accomplishment.

Many volunteer managers who do measure performance tend to measure the wrong things. They keep track of things like hours spent or miles driven or client contacts made. These measures tend to lack meaning because they do not really tell us whether the volunteer is accomplishing anything of value. They are not really measures of whether the result is being achieved. You can determine whether you have made this type of mistake, by examining the measures of performance and asking, "If all these were performed as specified, would it still be possible that the volunteer has not achieved any change or improvement in the clients?"

To determine how to measure a given result, involve the volunteers who do the job. Ask them these two questions:

"What information would tell us if you are succeeding in achieving results?"

"How could we collect this information?"

Measuring performance makes possible the setting of records. Records are tremendously motivating. People daily do ridiculous things to set records, such as making an omelette that weighs four tons. If people will spend time and effort to do such absurd things, imagine what productive work they might do if there were records to set.

Volunteer Job Descriptions

Commonly, the volunteer job is written up in the format of a job or position description, much like that prepared for paid staff position, but focusing much more on the results that you want the volunteer to accomplish. This written description will both provide a summary of the work and activities to be performed by the volunteer and function as an instrument utilized in supervision and evaluation of the volunteer.

The discipline of writing a good job description is a useful one. In a strange way, job descriptions can be much more important for volunteer staff than for paid staff. Paid staff are accustomed to 'learning' their job by osmosis - coming to work and spending time watching what is happening and determining what they should do. For a volunteer, this learning time period may be excessive, since two weeks of on-the-job learning can easily translate into several months of 'volunteer time.' Unless the agency is prepared for the volunteer to begin work immediately, and has prepared suitable instructions, the volunteer can become discouraged before even beginning work. A job description which accurately represents the effort to be done can serve as a method for readying the agency for the appearance of the volunteer. If you discover that either you or the staff with whom the volunteer will be working cannot put together a precise job description, then it would be better to re-initiate the process of job development than to recruit a volunteer for a position that does not really exist yet.

Determining Results and Measurements

Let's look at a real example of how these four principles can make a job interesting. It comes from a volunteer program whose main purpose is to do household chores for handicapped and elderly people who would otherwise be institutionalized. Originally, the volunteer job description wasn't even in writing. Volunteers were simply told to do whatever cleaning and home maintenance the paid social worker deemed necessary. They program was plagued with a high turnover rate, as volunteers often found the work more unpleasant than they had expected. In terms of our four criteria for a Good Job, the volunteers did have turf - their clients were their own and no one else's. However, they had no control over what they did, as the social worker limited them to a certain list of tasks. There was no clear result that they could see, and they were measured only by whether they accomplished their assigned activities.

In re-designing the job, staff and the volunteer manager sat down with a group of volunteers to define results and measures. At this two-day meeting, two results were identified. The first was that clients would be able to stay in their homes as long as they had no serious medical problems that made institutionalization necessary. This result was easily measured by the number of non-medical institutionalizations. Such a result didn't seem enough for the volunteers involved, however, since they felt they could easily achieve it and still do a lackluster job. They suggested that a second result be included, that client houses be clean. This brought up the problem of how to measure whether a house was clean, since people have different standards of acceptable cleanliness. After much discussion, the group finally decided that the client should be the one to determine if the house was clean or not. The final statement of this second result was "client will be satisfied with the cleanliness of their homes."

The next step was to determine how to measure this second result. The two key questions were asked: "What information will tell us that we are succeeding in doing a good job?" and "How will we collect it?" As in most cases, the answer was implied by the result statement itself. The information required was the opinion of the client. Volunteers could get this information informally by asking the client at the end of their visit. The program also solicited the opinions of clients on a more formal basis, through a monthly survey. The results of this survey, in terms of numbers of satisfied clients, was given back to the volunteers.

Within the framework of these results, the volunteer was then given the authority to do the thinking necessary to achieve them. Instead of the social worker figuring out what needed to be done, the volunteer was given the responsibility to work this out with the client. The volunteer's success in fulfilling this responsibility was measured by the degree to which the volunteer achieved the two results. Where volunteers were having difficulty achieving client satisfaction, they naturally turned to their supervisor for help and advice as to what they should do differently.

This change in the way the job was defined had a transforming effect on all concerned. The social workers were relieved of the enormous burden of determining what chores needed to be done for each client and were able to concentrate on actually doing social work. This made them happier and, because they were able to work personally with isolated clients, it also resulted in a reduction in the number of clients who complained because complaining was the only way they know how to cope with their loneliness.

The volunteers got greater satisfaction from their work, as they were responsible not just for doing odious chores but for keeping their clients out of a nursing home—a much more rewarding role. They had the authority to devise ways of accomplishing this and of cleaning the homes to the clients' satisfaction. Because of all this, volunteer turnover was greatly reduced, dropping almost to zero, and the agency developed a statewide reputation for good client service.

The volunteer manager's role also changed. Instead of being the person who assigned volunteers to clients and then tried desperately to keep them interested in doing the task (by recognition dinners, certificates of appreciation, motivational talks, and other highly time-consuming measures), the volunteer manager was now a resource person volunteers sought out whenever they perceived they were not achieving adequate results. The amount of time spent in recruiting was greatly reduced due to lack of turnover, as was the amount of time spent in 'motivating' volunteers.

Elements in a Job Description

A good job description will contain the following elements:

Title:
What the job will be called, or what position is being offered.

Purpose:
What the job is to accomplish. This is the most important part of the job description.

Activities:
Examples of what might be done to accomplish the purpose, given as suggestions, not requirements.

Qualifications:
What skills, attitudes, knowledge are desired.

Timeframe:
Estimated number of hours, length of commitment, and flexibility in scheduling.

Site:
Location of work.

Supervision:
Reporting requirements and supervisory assignment.

Benefits:
Training, insurance, parking, etc.

The precise format by which these are communicated is not important. What is important is that all of the elements be addressed and that, in particular, a well-thought purpose be defined for the volunteer.

Negotiating and Updating

While the job description ought to be formally constructed before seeking to recruit volunteers, it should not be considered an immutable 'finished' document.

In practice, the job description should in fact undergo considerable revision and change. It should change during the screening and interviewing process, as the interviewer attempts to 'match' the job to the needs and interest of the potential volunteer. It should change after the volunteer has been accepted and begins work, as the volunteer has the opportunity to enact alterations suggested by greater familiarity with the actual work to be done. And it should change as the volunteer continues to work, being updated as the skills of the volunteer improve and additional responsibilities are given.

The job description should be a fluid document that expresses what the volunteer and the agency are attempting to accomplish together; it should change and develop as that joint purpose alters.

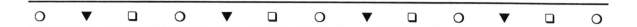

○ ▼ ❑ ○ ▼ ❑ ○ ▼ ❑ ○ ▼ ❑ ○

Chapter Four
Recruitment

Meeting the Needs of Potential Volunteers

Recruitment is the process of seeking volunteers who might want to help meet the needs of the agency and its clients, who will want to perform the work represented in the Circle of Staff Needs, and who are attracted by the result or purpose outlined in the volunteer job description. You might picture the process of recruitment as an exercise in first creating a *Circle of Volunteer Needs*, representing those things which a volunteer might want from an agency, including such items as interesting work, flexibility, recognition, etc:

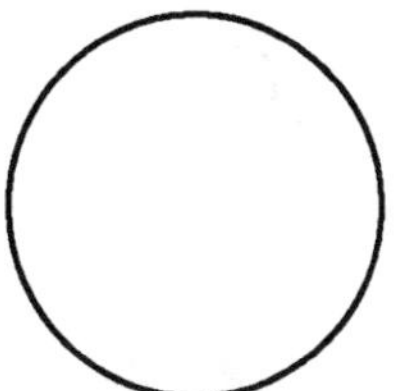

This circle can be constructed for every individual volunteer, because each of them will have a slightly different mix of needs and motivations.

The recruitment process then becomes an effort to identify and locate those volunteers whose circles of needs are congruent with what the agency needs and wants, i.e., whose motivational needs can be met by the volunteer position which the agency has to offer. It is essential, however, to remember that the recruitment process begins, and in many ways hinges upon, the creation of a good volunteer job. If you ask a person "What would it take to get you to volunteer some of your time for this agency?", the answers which you get tend not to be about the recruitment technique involved, but about the type of job you are asking them to do. Nearly all will say something like, "It would have to be a challenging job", or "It would have to be something that I felt was worthwhile", or "It should be work that would improve my skills". Attempting to recruit without first having developed worthwhile jobs is equivalent to attempting to sell a non-existent product—most people are unlikely to buy it.

The Recruitment Funnel

The recruitment process might also be pictured as a "Funnel". It is the procedure of identifying and separating from the entire universe of potential volunteers (the whole population of your community) those persons who best might fit the needs of the agency.

The utility of this metaphor is as follows:

Volunteer agencies may suffer from two very different types of recruitment problems. One problem, which is universally feared by new volunteer managers, is that of not having enough volunteers. The second problem, which is much more subtle and yet much more common, is of not having enough of the 'right' volunteers, and, indeed, of usually having too many of the 'wrong' ones.

Effective recruitment consists of attracting just enough of the right volunteers.

This distinction is an important one, with significant implications for a volunteer manager. Inexperienced volunteer managers often think that it is desirable to have large numbers of potential volunteers seeking to work with a program. Unfortunately, in practice a surplus of volunteers is extremely detrimental. If you advertise for volunteers for a position, and have only room for two volunteers, what do you do if 20 show up? Initially you must expend significant amounts of time in the screening and interviewing process, determining which of the volunteers should be accepted. Then you must 'reject' most of the volunteers, risking the prospect of their becoming resentful. The only thing worse than having to reject these volunteers is accepting their service when you don't really have work for them to do, at which point they will really become convinced that both you and the agency are incompetent.

Recruitment, then, becomes a matter of proportion, balancing the need for applicants with the work required in separating the qualified from the unqualified.

How to Recruit Volunteers

There are two different types of recruitment processes utilized by volunteer-involved agencies. Each is quite different in what it seeks to accomplish and in what it is effective in accomplishing.

"Warm Body Recruitment" is the first type of recruitment process.

Warm Body Recruitment

Warm Body recruitment is effective when you are trying to recruit for a volunteer position that can be done by most people, either because no special skills are required or because anyone can be taught the necessary skills in a limited amount of time. Examples of jobs suitable for Warm Body Recruitment include a "hugger" at a Special Olympics event or a worker at an Information Booth. Warm Body Recruitment is particularly effective when seeking large numbers of volunteers for short-term simple jobs, such as those who would help at a special weekend event.

Methods for Warm Body Recruitment

Warm Body Recruitment consists of spreading the message about the potential volunteer position to as broad an audience as possible. The theory is that somewhere among this audience will be those who find this position interesting.

The primary methods for Warm Body Recruitment are:

1. Distribution of agency brochures, bill stuffers, or posting of job descriptions.
2. Use of mass media: TV or radio PSAs; newspaper ads.
3. Speakers Bureau: giving talks to community groups.
4. Word of Mouth: encouraging staff and volunteers to talk about volunteering.

The limits on Warm Body Recruitment are primarily financial, since one is constrained by the expense necessary to produce and distribute recruitment materials.

Targeted Recruitment

The second type of recruitment process is called "Targeted Recruitment."

Targeted recruitment is desirable when the job that must be done is not general in nature, but requires a more limited skill or attitude which is not common in the population. This could involve an educational skill (ability to do computer programming), a time availability (ability to work between 9am and 5pm on weekdays) or an attitude (capable of dealing with emotionally disturbed children).

Targeted recruitment involves a different conceptual process, one in which the volunteer manager must work through a series of questions designed to narrow the population who might be recruited to more manageable proportions:

1. What is the job that needs to be done?

As stressed above, it is the job, the opportunity to do something that meets the volunteer's motivational needs, that is the key to attracting most individuals. A general message, such as "Volunteers are needed at the Crisis Clinic", doesn't let anyone know what volunteers do there. As such, the message doesn't indicate to a potential volunteer that there is anything to do which they might find interesting.

Volunteer managers who send such a general message tend to do so for one or two reasons. The first is that it is so obvious to everyone in the agency what volunteers do that they assume the entire community is familiar with those efforts as well. If the agency does a good job of community education, this may well be so, but potentially valuable volunteers may not yet have gotten the message.

The second reason volunteer managers send general messages is that there are so many things volunteers do at the agency. As we will see in the next few sections, however, an effective recruitment effort is targeted to different segments of the population. Different jobs in an agency appeal to different people who have motivational needs. By targeting our campaign on different groups, we can stress particular jobs that appeal to those groups and avoid the flabbiness of a message that mentions no attractive jobs.

2. Who would want to do the job that needs to be done?

This is a question that most of us don't ask because we have had experience with successful volunteers from a variety of backgrounds. It is easier, however, to recruit the right person for the job if we have answered this question, because it is easier to target our message to the needs of that particular group. Messages sent to the community in general have to apply to everyone and often wind up speaking to no one in particular.

Ask yourself if there is a certain type of person who is being sought. Do you want someone from a particular age group? Do you want someone of a particular sex or ethnic background? Do you want someone with certain professional skills? The answers to these questions may be multiple—we may want young, old, and middle-aged people, for example. But if we have reached this conclusion in a thoughtful way (rather than merely saying, "We'll take any age group."), we can then begin to target a recruitment campaign on each of these groups, with a slightly different message to each.

The advantage of sending a slightly different message to each group is that we have a better chance of speaking directly to that group's motivational needs. We will therefore tend to get a larger percentage of people from each group to consider volunteering for our agency than we otherwise would. For example, if we identify newcomers to town as a potential group of volunteers, we might stress jobs in which they can get to meet new people, and our volunteer recruiting efforts would spotlight efforts in which people work as teams. If we identify harried executives as potential volunteers, on the other hand, we might stress jobs that can be done conveniently, even at home, and which have a fixed end point.

3. Where will we find them?

Once we have determined who we are trying to recruit, we can ask "Where will we find them?" If we are after a certain type of professional, are there professional societies or clubs where such people might be found? If we are after members of a given age group or a certain minority group, are there places where groups of such people gather? Where do they shop? Where do they worship? Where do they go for recreational activity? Again, if we simply begin trying to recruit anyone in the general community, the answer to this question is 'everywhere'. This answer makes our job a little more difficult because it will be harder to focus our recruitment efforts. People who are everywhere are also nowhere in particular.

The answer to the question "Where will be find them?" has a lot to do with the recruitment methods we will employ. For example, if we are trying to recruit "Yuppies" we might see about putting advertisements on grocery bags in upscale supermarkets or put flyers on the windshields of BMWs. If we are recruiting teenagers with time of their hands, we might set up a booth at the beach. Several volunteer programs have recruited single people by advertising in singles bars. If the potential volunteers live in a particular neighborhood, we might go door-to-door (a technique often used by volunteer fire departments).

This question also might lead us to speak to certain groups. Such groups might be formal or informal, and our talk to them might be a prepared speech or casual conversation. Communities tend to be made up of circles of people — social groups, groups of employees, clubs, professional organizations, etc. In identifying who we are after and where they are to be found, we move toward identifying the circles of people we want to reach in order to present our recruitment message.

People also belong to readership, listening, and viewing groups. If you are going to use the media in your campaign, you need to select which media to use based on the profile of its listeners/viewers/readers. Any newspaper, radio station or television station can supply you with such information.

4. How should we go about communicating with them?

As indicated above, once we have listed some locations where people can be found, the fourth step is to ask "How will we communicate our recruiting message to them?" This step is implied by the previous one, and if you have done a good job of figuring out where they can be reached, developing a message is easy.

In general, the most effective means of recruiting a volunteer are those in which two-way communication is possible. The best form is communication from a current volunteer or board member, since they are attributed with purer motives than those of paid staff. (There is always the possible, subconscious suspicion that the paid person is trying to get the potential volunteer to do some of the work so that the staff does not have to.)

One of the weaknesses of having no particular target group in mind is that it is difficult to use methods that involve two-way communication when you are trying to communicate with the general populace. If we are trying to recruit "members of the general community" who are "everywhere" we have to fall back on one-way communication such as direct mail, press releases, posters, public service announcements, grocery bag messages, newspaper ads, handbills or talk-show appearances. Such efforts do succeed in recruiting volunteers, but they are less efficient in recruiting effective, dedicated volunteers than those methods in which a potential volunteer can ask questions and in which we can speak directly to the candidate's own needs and skills.

People volunteer only because they want to. Helping a person see that she can do something that she wants to do is easiest when a two-way conversation can take place. Therefore, while you should include easy and inexpensive methods of recruiting volunteers in any recruitment drive, you will be most effective if you put an emphasis on one-to-one conversations and on talking to groups small enough to get a good two-way conversation going.

Recruiting through such methods is a more labor-intensive way of going about it than the one-way communication type of campaign. Again, this means involving other people in the recruitment process. It means the volunteer coordinator needs to manage the recruiting effort, not do it all herself.

5. What are the motivational needs of these people?

It is important that the recruitment message speak directly to the motivational needs of the potential volunteer. It must appeal to the reason the volunteer wants to do the job. If, for example, we are going to target newcomers to town in our recruitment campaign, we might surmise that one of their motivational needs would be to make new friends. We would then make sure that our recruitment campaign includes the information that the volunteer would meet lots of friendly, interesting people while he does the valuable work we are asking of him.

In addition to doing something worthwhile, each individual has a complex of other motivations for volunteering. Some of the common ones are listed below:

- To "get out of the house"
- To get to know important people in the community
- To establish a "track record" to help them get a job

- To make a transition from prison, mental illness or other situation to the "real world"
- To "test the water" before making a career change
- To make new friends
- To be with old friends who volunteer at the agency
- To develop new skills
- To gain knowledge about the problems of the community
- To maintain skills they no longer use otherwise
- To impress their present employer
- To spend "quality time" with some members of the family by volunteering together
- To gain status
- To escape boredom
- To feel a part of a group

When we identify our target groups, we can then guess at which of these or other needs will be most important to individuals in that group. We can then send a message which speaks directly to those needs. People might respond to messages stressing motivators as diverse as patriotism, a need to protect their families, or a need to advance their careers. Here, for example, is a very effective ad designed to recruit macho males:

> *"Men wanted for hazardous journey. Small wages, bitter cold, long months of complete darkness, constant danger, safe return doubtful. Honor and recognition in case of success."*

This speaks effectively to a person who has a need to feel he is tough, and who has a need to test himself against very demanding physical circumstances. A similar appeal was used successfully by a volunteer director who had been having a very difficult time trying to find people to escort children to school through gang-infested housing projects.

6. What will we say to them?

The sixth major step is to develop an effective recruitment message. Often, no thought is given to this at all—we just send people out to talk about what the agency does and about the kinds of volunteer jobs we want people to do. By doing this, we needlessly reduce the number of people who will respond to us.

The Need

An effective recruiting message has three parts, the first of which is a statement of the need. The statement of need tells the volunteer why the job he will be doing is important. Most recruiting messages seldom talk about why we want the person to do a particular job. They only talk about the activities the person will be performing. This leaves it up to the person being recruited to figure out what the need for those activities is.

The need usually refers to something that exists in the community, not something that exists inside the agency. "Our senior center needs volunteers to help cook hot meals for seniors one day a week" is not the kind of statement we are referring to. The problem with such a statement is that it conjures up only the picture of sweating over a hot stove, and there are few people who are likely to be excited about doing that. Many, however, would find their interest engaged by the opportunity to do something to prevent senior malnutrition. By including a statement of need in the recruitment message, we show people how they can help solve a problem rather than merely do some activities.

Oftentimes, for volunteers involved in direct service, the need will be the need of the clients to be served. A few such statements of need are listed in an abbreviated form below:

Senior Nutrition Site volunteer:

> "Many elderly in our community cannot afford to get a balanced diet and are suffering from malnutrition."

Hospital volunteer:

> "Many patients in the hospital for long stays are lonely and depressed."

Crisis clinic volunteer:

> "Some people in our community suffer from mental fear and anguish so intense that they do harm to themselves and to other people."

Literacy volunteer:

"Many people from all walks of life are unable to take advantage of the full benefits of our society because they are unable to read or write."

Girl Scout leader:

"Many girls grow up without the self-confidence and other skills to become competent, successful adults."

Fire department volunteer:

"People in outlying areas who have heart attacks cannot be reached from the main station in time to save their lives."

Mental health receptionist:

"Clients coming into the center are often embarrassed, confused and uneasy."

Art museum docent:

"Many people who visit the museum would like to know more about the exhibits. Sometimes their lack of knowledge causes them to miss a great deal of the meaning and beauty of the exhibits, and their interest in returning to the museum wanes."

Friendly visitor:

Some seniors live in housing developments with little or no contact with other people or the outside world. They are sometimes, sick, in need of assistance, or in some instances dying, and no one is aware of their plight.

Such statements naturally lead the potential volunteer to think "That's terrible. Somebody should do something about that." Once the person is thinking this way, recruiting them is as easy as showing them that they can be somebody. Here is a very powerful and simple recruitment message, based on this principle:

"People are hungry.
Somebody should do something about that"
Be somebody. Call (our agency).

In responding to statements of need such as those above, the volunteer is directly answering the needs that the agency itself exists to address. On the other hand, some volunteers are recruited to do things that do not directly affect the agency's main work. Some clerical types of volunteer jobs, for example, exist to meet the needs of staff or of the agency more than they do the needs of the clients or the community.

In talking about the need in such circumstances, it is important to talk about the needs of the staff in the context of their work in meeting the needs of the community. A few examples are listed below:

Voluntary Action Center clerk/typist:

"When people call up wondering what they can do to help make the community a better place, staff are sometimes limited in their responses because the information we have is not filed systematically and not typed."

United Way envelope stuffer:

"A key part of our being able to support agencies who are working to solve the problems of our community is a direct mail appeal, which is hindered by lack of staff time to stuff and address the envelopes."

Public television phone worker:

"Citizens who enjoy the programming provided only on public television depend on pledge drives to keep us on the air, yet we have far too few staff to mount such drives."

Community action agency bookkeeper:

"In order to continue our efforts to improve the lives of the poor, we must account for our grants properly, a skill none of our staff have."

The statement of need should lead the potential volunteer naturally to the conclusion that something ought to be done about it. In one-to-one or small group situations, the recruiter can stop at this point to check to see if the potential volunteers agree that this is a need worth doing something about. Often, in such situations, the potential volunteer may stop to remark on the seriousness of this situation. Once you get a volunteer thinking that somebody should do something about the problem, recruitment is as easy as showing them that they are somebody.

Returning to our example of the senior center, the recruiter might ask the potential volunteer if he was aware that many seniors in the community were unable to afford nutritionally balanced meals and were suffering from malnutrition. She might include some anecdotal evidence or some statistics, though these are often less compelling in conversation than stories about actual people. If he doesn't say anything, she might ask what he thinks about it.

The Job

All this then leads naturally to the second element of an effective recruitment message, which is to show the volunteer how he or she can help solve this problem. In other words, now is the time to talk about the job description or what we want the volunteer to do. By describing these activities in the context of the need, we make our recruitment message more powerful. If we merely jump in and talk about the activities without also defining the need, some people will be able to figure out why such activities are important, but others won't. By making the assumption that people will see why the work is worth doing, we needlessly screen out people who would like to give their time to a worthwhile effort but aren't able to see why this job is important. Using our example, the potential volunteer might be quite eager to help out in the kitchen to help overcome the problem of malnutrition, while he may be totally uninterested in the job if it is merely described as cooking, busing dishes and serving meals.

When talking to a potential volunteer about a job, the recruiter should attempt to help the volunteer see himself doing the job. People only do what they can picture themselves doing, so we need to make our description of the job as vivid as possible. Talk about the physical environment, the people they will meet, the minor details that create a full picture of the environment the volunteer will encounter.

The picture we create should stress the positive elements of the job in order to encourage the person to volunteer, but it should also be honest. Although recruiting does have something in common with selling a product, we must refuse to sell the volunteer experience if we think the volunteer will not be satisfied with it. If we were trying to sell the volunteer a new truck, we might exaggerate the positive aspects of the purchase, but in recruiting we are trying to show him that he can do something he wants to do. If he volunteers under false pretenses, we will only waste a lot of time in training and trying to motivate a person who will probably not last long in the job.

In addition to painting a picture of the job to be done, we want to put the volunteer in the picture. The recruiter should always talk about what "you" will be doing, not about what "a volunteer" will do. A good technique to use in this regard is to ask the person some questions about how he would react in certain job situations. These situations should be easy and pleasant ones to handle, not questions such as "What will you do if a client throws up on you?"

The questions should also assume that the person is indeed going to volunteer. Avoid saying "If you decide to do this." Instead ask questions such as:

> *"What hours will be best for you?"*
>
> *"What appeals to you most about this work?"*
>
> *"What can we do to make the experience fun for you?"*
>
> *"Will you be able to attend our staff meetings?"*

Benefits

In addition to talking about the need and the job, the message should also talk about how the experience will allow the volunteer to meet the motivational needs he brings to the job. This third part of the message, the benefits, helps people see how they can help themselves by doing activities that help the agency serve the community.

To be as effective as possible, the recruitment message needs to show the potential volunteer that whatever combination of need she has can be met by the agency. This section of the message is particularly important in recruiting volunteers for clerical or staff support jobs, such as the legendary envelope stuffer. People don't volunteer to stuff envelopes because of the sheer joy of it or for the satisfaction of creating mountains of mail. They do it for some other reason, the most common one being the pleasure of socializing with a group of other people while they do this important but not very exciting task.

If the recruitment message is presented in a one-way format, it should list some benefits the volunteer coordinator thinks will appeal to the target group. If it is being presented in two-way format, where the recruiter has an opportunity to talk to potential volunteers about their needs, skills and desires, the benefits can be tailored specifically to the audience.

Because each volunteer has a different combination of motivations for volunteering, the recruiter needs to know something about the person in order to do the most effective job of encouraging him to volunteer. If the person wants to gain job experience, we want to make sure we stress jobs that allow him to do that, for example.

If the recruiter doesn't know the person she is trying to recruit, and if she is able to arrange the circumstances to allow for it, she should spend some time with the person to find out what kind of benefits might appeal to him, perhaps suggesting a few from the list on pages 47 - 48. This situation also provides the opportunity to identify some things the potential volunteer is concerned about and enjoys doing, and other clues to what it is he wants to do. This may lead to the establishment of new volunteer job opportunities.

For example, a person who wants to help the aforementioned senior center might have a hobby of photography. As the recruiter talks to the person about helping out in the kitchen (which is what the agency wants him to do), she may notice that he is only mildly interested in that particular job. When she talks to him about photography, however, his interest perks up. She might then ask if he would be interested in using his photographic skills to help the center.

If the recruiter learns what kinds of benefits are important to the volunteer, it is important that these be communicated to the volunteer coordinator so she can make sure the volunteer's experience fulfills his expectations. One cause of volunteer turnover is that volunteers don't get the things they volunteered to get. They volunteered to be with friends and got assigned to different shifts; they volunteered to get involved in a regular, soothing, non-stressful activity and were given a high-risk task; they volunteered to learn new skills and never got the chance to do anything beyond what they already knew; they volunteered to impress their employer and never got a letter of thanks sent to the employer; and so on. The information obtained from effective recruiting is the same information that can be used in successful volunteer retention.

The statement of benefits, like the statement of need, is often omitted by recruiters, perhaps because they would like to ascribe purer motives to volunteers or because it is so obvious to them. Leaving it out, however, needlessly reduces the number of people we can attract to assist our agency.

Stating the need, the job and the benefits is essential if we are to have the best chance of recruiting as many effective people as possible. Regardless of the types of recruitment methods you use, tell the people what the problem is (the need); show them how they can help solve it (the job); and tell them what they will gain (the benefits) in the process. Even if the space is limited, include all three. Here, for example, is a four sentence recruitment message that fit on a poster:

Children are being abused.
You can help by offering temporary shelter.
And help yourself at the same time.
Call (our agency phone number)

7. Who will do it?

The seventh step in preparing an effective recruitment campaign is to consider "Who will do the recruiting?" This is where we decide how to get more two-way communication into our recruiting effort and who will take the responsibility for creating posters, contacting radio stations and other forms of one-way communication.

As indicated above, the most effective people are often those who are volunteers or board members of the agency. In order to insure their effectiveness, however, we need to be sure they know that this is their responsibility, who they are supposed to recruit, where to find those people, how they are supposed to do it, and what they are supposed to say. In short, they need to be well equipped by staff to do the most effective job possible.

An often overlooked and extremely effective resource is a person who is recruited specifically to recruit volunteers. If you are looking for volunteers from the workplace, for example, an effective first step is to recruit an employee whose volunteer job is to identify potential volunteers within the company and recruit them for jobs they would want to do. Such a person can play this role year-round, thus providing more flexibility than other means of recruitment. Every time a need for a volunteer arises, the volunteer coordinator can put the word out through the volunteer recruiters. Those people can then approach people they know who might be interested in the new opportunity to volunteer.

An effective volunteer program might have volunteer recruiters in a variety of the groups that make up the community at large. Such a network, once established, enables the volunteer coordinator to use the most effective form of recruitment—face-to-face contact with someone you know—in a systematic and easy way. A good way of setting up such a system is to have staff, board members and other volunteers think about people they know in the various community groups who might be willing to volunteer their time in this way. These people can then be brought together for a training session.

Although a lot of effective, person-to-person recruiting "just happens," we can make a lot more of it happen by systematically encouraging it. Everyone involved in the organization, both volunteers and staff, should understand what their recruiting responsibilities are within the framework of the overall plan. Each time a need for a new volunteer arises, the volunteer coordinator prepares a job description, and a rough statement of the need and possible benefits. This can be communicated to all staff, board members and present volunteers (especially those recruited for this purpose) so that they might begin looking, among the people they know, for good candidates.

8. How will they know what to do?

The last step in preparing for the recruitment effort is to train those who will be delivering the recruitment message. If you follow the principles described above, this means training everyone involved with the agency. Everybody knows potential volunteers; it's just a matter of getting them to think about asking people they know to make a commitment to solving agency needs and of equipping them to make a coherent case for doing so.

In general, training should cover the participants' role in the recruitment process and provide adequate opportunity for them to role-play their presentation of the recruitment message. Ways of making sure participants learn from the training experience are covered in the chapter on training.

Assessing Your Recruitment Plan

To sum it up, keep these questions in mind as you prepare for your next recruitment campaign:

- What is the job that needs to be done?
- Who would want to do this job?
- Where will we find them?
- How should we go about communicating with them?
- What are the motivational needs of such people?
- What will we say to them?
- Who will do it?
- How will they know what to do?

Taking the care to answer these questions thoughtfully will help you to manage a more effective recruitment campaign.

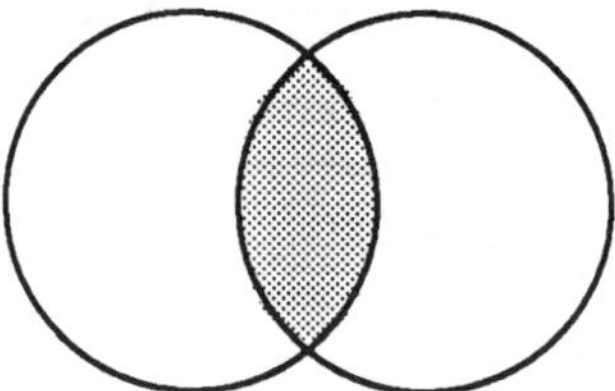

The key is to attempt to match the potential needs of some type of potential volunteer with the needs of the agency, as represented in the job which it has to offer. By focusing on features of the job—who would be best capable of performing the work it requires, who might benefit from participating in it—a plan of recruitment can be put together which focuses on a volunteer more likely to want and to be successful at that particular job.

Closing

Most volunteer organizations tend to focus on recruiting, as though an infinite supply of volunteers could solve anything. In truth, recruitment will not be a problem for your program if you follow two simple principles:

- Think broadly in terms of the possibilities within your agency in regard to the potential use of volunteers, and then think narrowly in terms of the message and methods you might utilize to find these volunteers.

- Have good jobs to offer, and be willing to be flexible in terms of the work and timeframe for accomplishing these jobs.

It is also important to remember that recruitment is actually a continuous process which lasts throughout your relationship with a volunteer. In essence, you need to think of recruiting that volunteer every time they show up for work, and motivating them to remain with your program by re-enforcing the original motivations which allowed you to involve them to begin with.

○ ▼ ❑ ○ ▼ ❑ ○ ▼ ❑ ○ ▼ ❑ ○

Chapter Five

Screening and Interviewing

The Purpose of Screening

Involvement of a volunteer requires both attracting that volunteer to the organization (by some type of recruitment procedure) and then negotiating with the volunteer to determine if there are some compatibilities of interests between the volunteer and the agency. This process of negotiation begins during the screening and interviewing process.

Since the process is one of negotiation it is important to remember that it ought to be a two-sided process, one in which compromises must be made on both sides, and in which everyone must win for the deal to go through. For an agency to assume that the purpose of screening is simply to 'announce' its requirements and expect that a volunteer will accept them is equivalent to entering into a negotiation with an inflexible position and telling the other side to 'take it or leave it.' The volunteer will rightly choose to simply leave it and find a more accommodating agency.

The principle idea in screening to is attempt to determine what the potential volunteer really wants and is interested in doing, and then to adapt that to what the agency can utilize productively. While the discussion may begin with a focus on a single job which has attracted the potential volunteer, it is important to remember that it may quite rightfully digress from that job, either through a process of expansion or through consideration of a completely different position.

○ ▼ ❑ ○ ▼ ❑ ○ ▼ ❑ ○ ▼ ❑ ○

What to Look for in Screening

There are three key things to accomplish or determine during the screening process:

Fit

"Fit" is the interpersonal matching of the needs and interests of the volunteer with the needs and interests of the agency. An examination of proper fit would include determining three items regarding the volunteer:

1. To what extent does the volunteer have both an interest in a particular job and the requisite qualifications to perform that job?
2. To what extent does the volunteer have other interests and abilities that might be used to create a different job for them?
3. To what extent does the volunteer have a 'rightness' for working well in a particular job environment.

In many cases, "Rightness", which involves the likelihood that the volunteer will fit comfortably into the agency working environment, will be the key predictive factor for success. 'Rightness' could involve questions of style (relaxed, frenetic), personality (neat, messy; introverted, extroverted), behavior (smoking, non-smoking) or other items which would affect how the volunteer will get along, both with the agency in general and with a particular staff group with whom they might be assigned. Very often these interpersonal relationship factors become more important than factors of technical qualification, which can be learned if the volunteer is willing to stay with the agency. Quite simply: a volunteer who is happy in their working environment will make the job happen; one who is unhappy will not try to.

Recruitment

During the process of the interview it is crucial to remember that the volunteer has not actually been 'recruited.' At this stage they have only been 'attracted' to the agency. One purpose of the screening interview is to give the volunteer time to make a more deliberate examination of what the agency has to offer and to continue to 'sell' the agency and its work to the volunteer. Equal time has to be given to focusing on 'why' a particular job is important and interesting, as well as to whether the volunteer would be right for that job. Never assume that just because a volunteer has come to the interview that they are already a part of the organization. If the screening interview is your first contact with the volunteer then it is important that the volunteer feel welcomed and wanted during the interview process, and does not feel as though they have been caught by an uncaring bureaucracy which is only interested in determining which Square Hole the volunteer should fill.

Marketing

The final element to determine during the screening interview is marketing information. The screening process is a good place to assess the effectiveness of your recruitment procedure. You can determine from potential volunteers the two key marketing questions about your volunteer program:

> *How are potential volunteers hearing of our volunteer opportunities?*
>
> *What about our agency is attracting them?*

The response to these questions will better enable you to evaluate and correct your recruitment efforts.

The Interviewing Site

The site for conducting the interviewing process will vary, but it is important during the interview that the volunteer feel a sense of privacy and comfort. Do not conduct the interview in a public place, or a shared office, since this will deter many volunteers from offering complete information about their backgrounds and their interests. None of us likes being eavesdropped on while discussing our personal lives.

Organize your own schedule so that you will not be interrupted during the interview, either by phone calls or by other staff. Besides disrupting the flow of the interview, the interruptions will give the impression to the volunteer that they are of a much lesser importance than your other work.

While face-to-face interviews are much preferable, there will be times when you will choose to conduct either a pre-interview by telephone, or where considerations such as geography or sheer numbers do not allow you to meet each potential volunteer in person. Deciding that it is appropriate to conduct an interview via telephone should depend upon the length of the time commitment you are asking from the volunteer (a year versus a one-time job at a special event), the level of responsibility (one member of a group of volunteers versus a committee chair) and the sensitivity of the work to be performed (a hugger at a Special Olympics game versus a volunteer matched one-to-one with a particular child). Whenever possible, conduct the interview in person, since the ability to watch the person you are talking with will give you a much better understanding of their reactions. If you cannot conduct the interview in person, attempt to compensate by arranging a bit more follow-up contact with the volunteer as soon as possible.

The Interviewer

The person conducting the interview ought to be selected for a number of qualifications:

1. The ability to explain the agency and its purposes, with a full knowledge of the possible work that a volunteer might perform and the ability to create a new volunteer position based on those needs.

2. The ability to follow an organized system during the interview, while understanding and relating to the potential volunteer and allowing their input, and the ability to negotiate with the volunteer.

3. The ability to say "No" gracefully, if the volunteer is not suitable for the agency.

You may want to consider involving staff during the interview process, or of setting up a procedure whereby staff are included in a second interview before the volunteer is assigned.

You will also want to consider utilizing experienced volunteers as interviewers. Volunteers who are familiar with the agency may actually make better interviewers than you. They are better able to relate to the situation of the potential volunteer and they have more credibility than do paid staff when explaining why it is desirable to work with the agency. Utilizing volunteer interviewers can also save you a lot of time for the jobs which ought to be done by you personally, such as working with staff in creating volunteer jobs.

Interviewing Process

The actual interviewing process should be considered as having three stages:

Pre-Interview Preparation

Before conducting an interview for a particular volunteer the interviewer should prepare questions that relate to two areas. The first set of questions should be open-ended in structure, and should be designed to elicit information about what the interests and motivation of the volunteer might be. Questions of this sort include the following:

> *"What would you like to get out of volunteering here? What would make you feel like you have been successful?"*
>
> *"What aspects have you enjoyed most about your previous paid or volunteer work?"*
>
> *"Would you rather work on your own, with a group, or with a partner? Why?"*
>
> *"What skills or strengths do you feel you have to contribute?"*

The second set of questions includes those which related to the skills and qualifications necessary to do a specific job. These must obviously be different for each position, and involve determination of availability, skills, experience, etc.

Interview

The actual interview will follow a process of become acquainted and comfortable with the volunteers, describing the process of screening and what the volunteer might expect, and then beginning the interviewing itself.

It is crucial to remember that this process belongs as much to the volunteer as it does to the agency. If there is a set time limit on the interview, make sure that you have allocated time for the volunteer to express concerns and questions. The interview is a mutual, not a unilateral, exchange process. It is a negotiation, not an interrogation.

The interview should conclude by telling the volunteer what they may expect to happen next, whether it is an immediate assignment, a re-contact date for later assignment, or the absence of a match with the needs of the agency.

Follow-up

Complete the interview process by following up on the placement of the volunteer. This could include checking references given by the volunteer, contacting staff about a need for a new position, etc.

What is crucial in this procedure is to do it as quickly as possible. The more time that is spent between the interview and the actual placement, the more likelihood that the volunteer will become disinterested. If there is a time delay between the interview and placement, attempt to keep in contact with the volunteer to assure them that they have not been forgotten.

Contracting

You may wish to consider initiating a process of 'contracting' with volunteers during the interviewing and matching process. 'Contracting' does not actually involve a formal legal document, as much as it does the signing by both the agency and the volunteer of a listing of the mutual commitment they are entering into. The agreement might specify the work which the volunteer is agreeing to perform, the timeframe, and the benefits and support which the agency agrees to provide the volunteer.

The purpose of the contract is to emphasize the seriousness of both the agency and the volunteer in entering into a relationship, and is not intended to convey a sense of 'legal' responsibility.

Exit Interviews

One sub-part of the interviewing process which should also be developed is that of the exit interview. An exit interview should be conducted with each volunteer who is separating from the program. The exit interview should determine why the volunteer is leaving and how other volunteers might be prevented from leaving. Some questions to ask during the interview include:

> *"Why are you leaving?"*
>
> *"What did you like best about volunteering with us?"*
>
> *"What suggestions would you make for changes or improvements in our volunteer effort?"*

You may also consider performing the exit interview via a written questionnaire, but should realize that this method will provide you with a lesser degree of useful information.

Closing

The screening and interviewing process is of vital importance and should receive the attention and time which this importance merits. Since this may be the agency's first contact with the volunteer, it should create a good impression on the part of the volunteer, a feeling that the agency wants and appreciates the services which the volunteer might provide. The interview should get things off on the right foot, and create a warm and friendly atmosphere.

The interview should also be a chance for creativity. Remember that the key is to work on matching the circles of interest of the volunteer and the agency, and to identify those areas of overlap which the volunteer really **wants** to do. Do not try to shove round pegs into square holes, work instead of developing a proper fit between the agency and the volunteer. Time spent getting the correct match will be saved later in a lessened need to supervision and trouble-shooting.

○ ▼ ❑ ○ ▼ ❑ ○ ▼ ❑ ○ ▼ ❑ ○

Chapter Six

Orientation and Training

Orientation

Orientation is the process of making volunteers understand and feel comfortable with the workings of the agency. It is designed to provide them with background and practical information that they will use to relate what they are doing with the overall functions of the agency and to better understand how they can contribute to the purpose of the agency. If the volunteer better understands the agency's systems, operations and procedures, then the volunteer will be better able to contribute productively.

Orientation content will vary from agency to agency, but should cover the following sorts of topics:

1. Description and history of the agency.
2. Description of programs and clientele.
3. Description of the volunteer program.
4. Sketch of organizational chart and introduction of key staff.
5. Timelines and description of major organizational events and activities.
6. Orientation to the facilities and equipment.
7. Description of volunteer procedures: recordkeeping requirements, benefits, training, supervision, etc.

The simplest way to develop the agenda for the orientation session is to ask yourself, "What would I like to know about this place in order to better understand how it works?" Remember that a volunteer who fully understands the organization can well serve as an effective communicator with the public about the worth of the organization, while a confused volunteer can present quite the opposite picture.

The orientation session is a useful place in which to involve staff people, who can provide overviews of their departments or programs.

Orientation may be distinguished from training in that it is usually more general in nature, while training should be tailored to a specific volunteer position.

Training

Training may be provided to volunteers in three formats: formal training session, coaching, or counseling.

Formal Training

Formal training for volunteers may be given to prepare them for a specific job. Crisis clinics, for example, provide volunteers with many evenings of training in how to deal with disturbed callers. One program that counsels delinquent children requires one evening per week of training for a year before the volunteer begins work with clients. Fire department volunteers typically attend training once a week to polish and expand their skills for as long as they are with the department.

Training may be delivered in a number of formats: lectures, readings, discussion, field trips, videos, panel discussions, demonstrations, role-playing, case studies, simulations, etc. It is common in a training session to employ a variety of techniques so as to better retain the attention of the audience.

There are two primary areas which it is essential to cover in developing volunteer training, regardless of the job for which the training is being provided.

The first area might be termed a description of the functions of the volunteer job. It would include training which communicates to the volunteer:

1. This is what you should do and accomplish in your job.
2. This is what you should not do.
3. This is what you should do if the following situation arises.

For example, a volunteer who is recruited to assist elderly clients in getting to medical appointments might be trained as follows:

1. ***Do***: be on time or notify the program coordinator 3 hours in advance; help patients in and out of the car; be familiar with the city; have an inspected automobile.

2. ***Don't***: volunteer to assist clients with in-home chores; offer to take clients to other appointments on an unscheduled basis or to take clients shopping; tell clients about the medical conditions of others.

3. ***If***: if there is a medical problem en route, go immediately to the nearest emergency room, the locations of which are marked on this map which we are providing you.

In essence you provide the volunteer with the collected experience in both successes and problems that previous volunteers have acquired.

The second areas might be termed a description of roles and responsibilities. It would include training which communicates to the volunteer:

1. This is who you will be working with and this is your role in the task.
2. This is their role.

For example, this could include telling volunteers who will be responsible for supervising them and to whom they will be reporting during their assignment. If the volunteer is working with a client in conjunction with other volunteers, it would include introducing the volunteer to the other workers and to what they are providing for the client.

The intent of training is to prepare the volunteer to perform the tasks to which they are assigned, and it should therefore inform them both of the formal techniques which they will need to know and of the network of relationships within which they will be working.

○ ▼ ❑ ○ ▼ ❑ ○ ▼ ❑ ○ ▼ ❑ ○

Coaching

Coaching follows a three step process to help volunteers acquire skills. Those steps are as follows:

1. A demonstration of the skill to be learned or improved.
2. Observation of the volunteer performing the skill.
3. Feedback and analysis.

The goal of the coaching process is greater volunteer autonomy and ability.

The volunteer director may use other staff to demonstrate the skill or may do it personally. In either case, it is important that the person demonstrating the skill explain why he is doing what he does as he does it. The point of the demonstration is not just to allow the volunteer to see what is done but to understand it.

To take an extremely simple example, if you were to demonstrate to a volunteer how to answer the agency telephone, you might follow these steps: First, have the volunteer watch as you answer the phone; Second, have the volunteer answer the phone while you watch; Third, have the volunteer answer the phone by himself for a while and then report his experiences.

EIAG Process

After each of these steps, we would want to make sure the volunteer learns from the experience. In this, we can be guided by a learning model that goes by the acronym **EIAG**. Although this doesn't spell anything, the four letters are the first letters in the four major steps people go through to learn things. If we keep these four steps in mind when we coach volunteers, we can make sure they learn the most from the coaching process.

Experience

The "E" in EIAG stands for experience. People learn from experience, but not always. Sometimes people have an experience over and over and never learn from it. When a brain learns from experience, it goes through the remaining three steps.

Identify

The "I" in EIAG stands for identify. If someone is going to learn from an experience, they must be able to describe what that experience was. In the simple example of learning to answer the phone listed above, some questions we might ask at the various steps to get someone to describe the experience are:

What did I do?

What did you do?

How did the other person react?

How have things been going for you?

What has been happening?

Analyze

The third step in learning from experience is to analyze it. If a person is to learn from the identified experience, he must be able to analyze why it happened the way it did. We want to get them to explore the factors in the situation that produced the experience. To continue our simple example, some questions we might ask to help the volunteer analyze the steps are:

Why did I begin by saying "Good morning."

Why did the caller get so upset with you?

Why have things been going so well?

Generalize

The "G" in EIAG stands for generalize. If a person is to learn anything useful from an experience, he must be able to come up with some general rule or principle that applies beyond the specific situation to other, similar situations. Again, an effective coach relies on questions in this step. Some examples are:

What will you do when you encounter a situation like this?

What would you do differently if you had to do it over again?

What will you do to make sure things continue to go so well?

○ ▼ ❑ ○ ▼ ❑ ○ ▼ ❑ ○ ▼ ❑ ○

An Example of EIAG

Let's see how this might work in a more complex example. As stated previously, coaching is particularly important with a volunteer who is new to a skill or concept. Imagine, for example, that you are a teacher of handicapped children and that you have a volunteer named Hank. You want Hank to help a child named Johnny learn to put his coat on and take it off. Although Hank has some experience in working with handicapped children, he has never done anything like this before. So you start by having Hank watch you conduct the program. Afterwards, you use the EIAG technique to discuss things with Hank. Some questions you might ask Hank include:

What did you see me do with Johnny? (identifying)

What problems did I encounter? (more identifying)

Why do you think these occurred? (analyzing)

What do you think you could do to avoid such problems? (generalizing)

What techniques seemed to work well? (more identifying)

Why did these techniques work better than others I tried? (analyzing)

Based on what you saw, what are some things you will avoid and some things you will do when you work with Johnny? (generalizing)

Once we are confident that Hank will be able to work with Johnny, we watch him carefully while he attempts to conduct the lesson. During this time, if it seems like Hank is doing something that will upset or harm Johnny in any way, we would of course interrupt and suggest a different course of action. Or we might take over the lesson again ourselves. In any case, after Hank's attempts, we would again ask questions to help him learn and grow from his experience:

How would you describe what happened? (identifying)

Why did you put your own coat on? (analyzing)

What were the strengths of your approach? (analyzing again)

Why did Johnny slap the applesauce out of your hand? (more analyzing)

Based on this insight, what will you do differently next time? (generalizing)

In the course of this, we may need to go back and demonstrate the skill ourselves, with Hank watching. We would then go back to watching him. Eventually, when we are comfortable that Hank has mastered the skill, we would allow him to work without us watching. Nonetheless, we would continue to check on his progress from time to time, using the EIAG questions to make sure he is continuing to grow in his abilities. The checking would include direct observation and reports from Hank. Eventually, we would get comfortable enough to rely simply on Hank's self-observations.

As you begin to use the EIAG model, it is important that the sequence of questions you use be natural. Sometimes we have a tendency to get locked into our prepared sequence of questions while a volunteer's response might naturally bring up other questions. If you have prepared a series of identification questions, don't ask them all in a row if you get an unexpected response on the first one. It might be better to go on and analyze that response than to proceed with your other questions.

The EIAG learning model is effective because it is a natural one. It merely makes conscious the subconscious method we employ all the time. When you employ it, you are merely making sure your volunteers complete all the steps in the learning process instead of leaving it up to chance that they will do it on their own.

Counseling

The goal of counseling is to assist the volunteer in solving a problem, or improving a behavior by getting the volunteer to take responsibility for the improvement. While coaching shows volunteers how they might improve, counseling helps volunteers discover how they might improve. The principle tool the effective manager employs in counseling is the Question.

A manager who knows that they will get the best results from empowered people uses a lot of questions in interactions with volunteers. Questions empower volunteers while leaving the questioner very much in control. The use of questions is a way managers can empower without losing control themselves.

Insecure, inexperienced supervisors think they should have all the answers. Whenever they interact with a volunteer, they feel that if they can't answer all the questions and have instant solutions for all the problems, they are failing. Insecure, traditional managers either make something up or make a snap decision when they are presented with a problem they really don't have an instant answer for. Or they tell the volunteer they will get back to him later.

The root of this behavior is the traditional manager's concern that the volunteers should have confidence in her and should respect her. By contrast, an effective manager is most concerned that volunteers should have confidence in themselves.

A volunteer whose supervisor has all the answers develops a sense of dependency on his boss. He therefore does not grow in his own capabilities. Further, since such managers often think it is their job to tell their volunteers what to do and how to do it, they tend to foster volunteer apathy and resentment, as described in the discussion of control. Volunteers in such circumstances tend to stagnate and decay, making it increasingly difficult for the supervisor to get good results.

The Counseling Process

When a volunteer encounters a problem in his work, the supervisor can use questions to help the volunteer do these things:

Identify the Problem

What is going wrong? What is happening?

Identify the Cause of the Problem

Why is the problem occurring? What is causing the problem? What factors in the situation are producing the problem?

Identify Alternatives

What are the alternatives we have in this situation? What else could we do? Have you considered this course of action? (making a suggestion) What would happen if we tried this?

Identify a Better Course of Action

What are the strengths and weaknesses of each alternative? What can you do to solve the problem?

Learn from Their Experience

What can you do differently in the future to avoid this problem?
What would you do differently if you had to do it over again?

Providing Counseling

As indicated above, it is fine to offer suggestions when counseling, offering additional information or courses of action that the volunteer might not see. In doing so, however, you should not be telling the volunteer what to do. Your role, in counseling, is to empower them to come up with their own solutions. In doing so, you need to get them to own ideas that come from you by having them analyze them. The conversation might go something like this:

"Have you considered this course of action?"

"Oh, so that's what you want me to do?"

"Not necessarily. Have you considered that?"

"No."

"What would happen if we did that?"

"I'm not sure."

"Do you see any risks of that approach?"

"No. I guess maybe it would work?"

"Why do you think it would work?"

"The clients wouldn't have to wait so long. And we would have more time to process their paperwork."

"So what do you think?"

"I guess it sounds like a good idea."

"Let's see how it goes."

Management Questions

A manager who knows that they will get the best results from empowered people uses a lot of questions in her interactions with volunteers. Questions empower volunteers while leaving the questioner very much in control. The use of questions is thus another way managers can empower while controlling. For each of the major management functions planning, enabling, and evaluating there are several key questions.

Planning Questions

The first set of management questions relate to planning. Planning is something managers should never do alone; they should always involve the people who will be carrying out the plan. Plans made by those who must implement the plan are based on more practical information and are pursued with the enthusiasm that comes from a feeling of ownership.

Sitting down with the people who will implement the plan, the manager facilitates the planning process by asking questions such as:

> *"What is our purpose?"*
>
> *"What new developments affect us?"*
>
> *"What are the trends?"*
>
> *"How can we take advantage of those trends and developments?"*
>
> *"What are the alternatives?"*
>
> *"What problems do you see?"*
>
> *"What opportunities do you see?"*

In groups larger than six or seven, the manager will find it easier to increase active participation by having small groups of volunteers meet to discuss each question and then report the results of their deliberations to the large group.

With the data generated in response to these questions, the manager brings the group to focus with questions such as:

"Based on all this, what should we be trying to accomplish?"

"What should our goals be for the upcoming period?"

In all of this, the manager need not play a purely facilitative role. She may have very strong opinions of her own concerning these questions. The manager should always sound out the group first, however. She should question them first, suggest second, and only third state her own opinion. Again, the idea is to empower the volunteers by making the ideas theirs, where possible, but the idea is also to stay in control and to set the most effective goals for the organization.

Once the goals are set by the planning group, one very powerful next move is to refer to each goal and ask "Who will take responsibility for this?" Again, the manager may have particular people in mind to do certain tasks and can certainly exercise her prerogative to assign responsibility. But where it is appropriate, asking for voluntary assumption of responsibility empowers the group and leads to more committed pursuit of the organization's objectives.

Other planning questions are appropriate after goals have been set and responsibility has been assigned or taken. At meetings with the responsible individual or team these questions can be asked:

> *"When can you have your plan to me?"*
>
> *"What is your target?"*
>
> *"How will we measure your success?"*
>
> *"What is your timetable?"*

At such meetings, enabling questions may also be appropriate. Perhaps the most powerful of the enabling questions is "Can you handle this responsibility?" Such a question challenges the volunteer and encourages self-reliance. In addition to being a good question when it comes to fixing responsibility for achieving part of the organization's planned results, it is an especially useful question to ask when delegating responsibility for a result, as in "John, I would like you to take responsibility for increasing our word-processing productivity through the purchase of new software. Can you handle it?"

This question may be followed up with "How will you go about it?" and/or "When can I see your plan?"

Motivational Questions

Other important enabling questions can be used in counseling and coaching volunteers on job performance and motivational issues. These include:

> *"How do you feel about your job?"*
>
> *"What are your frustrations?"*
>
> *"Do you know what you want to achieve in your job?"*
>
> *"What do you need to do your job better?"*
>
> *"Would you like some increased responsibility?"*

Other questions enable the manager to help volunteers see the connection between doing a good job and growing in their careers. By showing the volunteer that she would like to help him succeed not only in the job but in his career as well, the effective manager doubles the volunteer's motivation. These questions include:

"Do you know what you want to achieve in your career?"

"How can I make your job a means of achieving your career goals?"

"How can I help you build a track-record of excellent performance that will further your career?"

Evaluation Questions

Earlier, we stressed the importance of the manager establishing checkpoints at which a volunteer's performance is reviewed (unless he is at level one on the control scale). At these review meetings, it is again important for the manager to have the right questions. These evaluating questions include:

"How would you describe your performance?"

"Are you on-target or off?"

"What happened?"

"What went wrong?"

"Why did you do so well?"

"If you had it to do over again, what would you do differently?"

"What can you learn from your experience?"

"How will you do better in the future?"

"If you were going to advise another person who was about to try to achieve this same target, what would you tell him?"

These questions help the volunteer to analyze his experience in trying to reach his targets. They also firmly establish that he is responsible for that performance, not his boss. These questions help the volunteer learn from that experience so he can do better in the future. This is true whether the volunteer is doing well or poorly. An effective manager wants her volunteers to be constantly improving because if they are growing in their abilities, the manager will get better and better results from them.

Other evaluating questions should be asked of the whole unit at least once a year to make sure the organization stays as effective as possible. These powerful questions include:

"What are some better ways of doing what we do?"

"How can we work smarter?"

"How can we make what we do obsolete?"

These evaluating questions lead naturally into a new round of planning questions.

It is important to remember that the types of questions we are talking about empower the volunteer. They tell him that we have confidence in his ability to think, to take responsibility, to be accountable. They treat the volunteer as an adult and increase his feelings of autonomy, equality, and self-worth. Other types of questions, while also establishing that the questioner is in control, belittle the volunteer. "Did you expect anyone would really want this done?" for example, is a question, but not the kind of question an effective manager uses; she wants her people to feel confident as they go about their duties, not diminished, angry, or afraid.

Closing

Regardless of whether you are utilizing formal training, coaching or counseling, remember that the point is to make sure that volunteers learn from the experience. The mix of methods which you choose may vary from volunteer to volunteer, and even will vary over the term of the volunteer's relationship with the agency.

You can determine whether the learning experience has been a successful one by asking questions of the volunteer following the training. Some useful questions include:

"What point sticks out in your mind?"

"Why is that point so important?"

"What did you hear that most appealed to you?"

"Why do you feel that way?"

"How can you use this information in your volunteer job?"

"What implication does this have for your ability to be successful in your work?"

You should remember that training of any kind is almost always viewed with approval by volunteers. One of the primary benefits you can give a volunteer is additional information, skills, or assistance in performing their work more productively. Do not hesitate to ask for an additional commitment or effort from the volunteer to obtain training, since most of them will regard it as well worth the effort. To the volunteer, your interest in better preparing or counseling them on their work is regarded as a recognition of the significance and importance of their contribution to the agency.

Chapter Seven

Empowering Volunteers

Being a Manager of Others

The role of the person who manages volunteers is to achieve planned results from the people she supervises. Put another way, the manager's job is not to do things directly but to make sure things get done. Or, to put it still another way, the manager's job is to do things that enable others to do the work.

One of the difficulties of succeeding in this job is that getting things done through others is an indirect way of working. Most people who become volunteer directors are used to doing things themselves. As we will see in this chapter, the instincts that serve one well in getting the work done directly are often counterproductive when it comes to getting things done through others.

Creating a Motivating Environment

We succeed in volunteer management primarily by creating conditions that encourage volunteers to want to do the work. By building a job around the volunteer's needs for volunteering, as described previously, we begin by placing the volunteer in a job he wants to do. Further, we tap the volunteer's need for achievement by making sure he has a result to achieve, thereby providing the volunteer with responsibility which is likely to be satisfying. In this chapter, we will look at tapping another need, the volunteer's need to feel in control of what he does. We tap this need through several techniques that empower the volunteer.

By empowering volunteers, what we are talking about is making them more autonomous, more capable of independent action. The wisdom of this approach is that it is easier to get good results from empowered people than it is from people who are dependent. We do this by giving them authority to decide, within limits, how they will go about achieving the results for which they are responsible. In this way, management becomes a source of help to the volunteer rather than a goad. This not only feels better for the volunteer but allows managers to spend less time worrying about the details of the volunteers work and more time to think strategically, to concentrate on grasping the opportunities that will never be seen if we are mired in the muck of day-to-day details.

Levels of Control

In giving people authority over the how of their jobs, the danger is that we will lose control, that we will create more chaos than anything else. This dilemma, giving the workers control over their own actions while insuring that the actions they take will lead to the results we are trying to achieve through them, is one of the most critical dilemmas to solve in management. It is resolved by recognizing that there are four degrees or levels of control a volunteer can exercise in pursuing each result. These levels of control define how much say the supervisor and the volunteer each have in deciding how each result is to be achieved.

1. The Authority for Self-assignment.

At this first degree of control, the volunteer has been given or has taken the authority to decide for himself what he does. The term "self-assignment" means that the volunteer is the source of his own assignments; they come from himself, not from others. When a volunteer is operating at this level, he sees what needs to be done, he does it, and that is the end of it. Many managers are of course justifiably nervous about giving volunteers this much control because if the volunteer sees the wrong things that need to be done, there may be some problems in achieving the desired results. There is also a great potential for chaos if everyone a manager supervises is given this much control.

2. The Authority for Self-assignment Provided Regular Progress Reports Are Received.

The second degree of control gives the supervisor a bit more insurance that the right things are being done. When a volunteer is operating at this level, he sees what needs to be done, he does it, but at some point, he tells the boss what he has done. This gives his supervisor some increased insurance that things will work out right in the end, because if she doesn't like what he has done, she can take steps to fix it. How often these progress reports are received depends on how anxious she is about her volunteer's performance in fulfilling a given responsibility. The more anxious she is, the more frequent the reports should be.

3. The Authority to Recommend Self-assignment.

If the supervisor is very anxious about the volunteer's performance, if, in other words, she is worried that she is going to have to take steps to "fix it" more often than she feels is tolerable either for her or for the organization, then she might want the volunteer to exercise still less control. When a volunteer is operating at this third level, he is still the source of his own assignments. In this case, however, he gets approval from the supervisor before he acts. Here the supervisor has still more control because if she doesn't like the recommended course of action, she can stop the person from doing anything before he does it. At this third level, as with level two, volunteers also provide progress reports once their recommendations are approved.

Just as level two contains gradations of control in the form of varying frequencies of reports, so level three comes in a variety of shades. In some cases, managers might want daily plans from some volunteers, perhaps in the form of a prioritized list of things to do. More generous portions of control at this level come in the form of plans for the month or plans for the quarter or an overall plan for achieving the target. These gradations depend on the supervisor's degree of anxiety about the volunteer's performance in pursuing the particular targets.

4. No Authority for Self-assignment.

If the boss is not only anxious about the volunteer's performance but downright psychotic, she might be tempted to allow him still less control, and the only place lower to go is the fourth degree of control. At this level, it doesn't matter whether the volunteer sees what needs to be done. He just does what he is told to do.

At this fourth level of control, the volunteer has no authority for thinking, for deciding what needs to be done. At level four, that responsibility is transferred up, away from the place where the work is actually done, to the management level. This inevitably produces more work for the manager, because whenever someone is unsure what to do next, the manager will be given the assignment, by the volunteer, to figure that out. The more people the manager supervises, and the more complex their jobs, the more such assignments she will receive every day.

Putting volunteers at level four produces more serious problems than this, however. For one thing, we reduce the amount of creative input we get from volunteers. Good ideas for improving services will seldom surface if the volunteer is not expected to think. As the pace of change in the world outside the organization accelerates, yesterdays practices become increasingly obsolete. Volunteers, partly because they are not submerged inside the organization eight hours each day, are a valuable source of perspective and innovation that we must take advantage of if we are to stay relevant.

Motivation and Control

The major cost organizations pay when they put people at level four, however, is that the need for control is a very important motivator. When people are denied control over what they do, they are told, in essence, that they are too stupid to figure these things out, that thinking is the province of the smart people, the people who make higher salaries. Workers tend to resent this. And when volunteers feel resentment, we have failed to create the conditions that get results through them. The job will soon cease to be one they "want" to do. And when volunteers don't want to do the job, they will tend to find other uses for their leisure time.

Even if they do stay around, because the volunteering satisfies some other motivator such as a sense of duty or a social need, the volunteer's dedication is sapped when he has no authority. When carrying out an assignment, a volunteer can work with maximum energy or he can go through the motions. And no matter how brilliant the original decision was, that decision is only as good as the decision the worker makes as to which of these two approaches he takes to carrying it out.

Negative Ways of Meeting the Need for Control

On occasion, volunteers may even play a game that paid people often play when they are at level four. This is most likely to arise when the volunteer has been with the agency for years, longer than the person who is supervising her. She may feel that she is more a part of the agency than the paid staff, and so is unlikely to drop out. But if she feels resentment for being told what to do, she get her revenge by doing exactly what she was told to do in such a way that everything gets screwed up. She then gets the sweet satisfaction of saying "I did what you told me to do, and look what happened."

At level four, then, people have a positive incentive to perform incompetently. It defends their egos to do so; it gives them back the sense of control that they lose when the boss tells them what they can and can't do. It allows a person to prove to their supervisor, and especially to themselves, that they cannot be controlled. By unwittingly giving their people this psychological reward for doing the work poorly, traditional managers have to spend a lot more effort to get good results.

All this said, it is nonetheless volunteers who are most often placed at level four. Because they come in irregularly, and because things may have changed dramatically in the agency since the last time the volunteer was present, there is a great tendency to design the volunteer experience in such a way that the volunteer shows up without any notion of what they might do that day and be directed to perform some duties by a paid person. When the volunteer does not show much enthusiasm or drops out, staff complain about their unreliability. On the contrary, if you do not meet a person's motivational needs, you can rely on them to drop out. Wise volunteer programs thus give volunteers something they own, as described in the chapter on job design, and they give them authority at levels three, two, or (rarely) one to decide how to fulfill their responsibilities. By empowering volunteers in this way, we allow them to feel a great sense of pride and personal effectiveness, a sense they may not get in the rest of their lives. The desire to continue to volunteer is thus kept very strong.

In sum, to get maximum effectiveness from our volunteers, we need to keep the authority to decide how to achieve their results in their hands. There are, however, two exceptions to this rule. The first is when they are in training, since a person who is new to the job may not know the job well enough to recommend what to do. The second instance is in an emergency. When time is short, there may not be enough time to wait for a recommendation, weigh it, express your concerns, and get a revised recommendation. Apart from these two times, however, we want to keep people above level four.

Climbing the Control Ladder

The remaining levels of control are a ladder for people to climb. When a person first comes on board, and we are satisfied that he knows the job well enough to make an intelligent recommendation, we start him at level three. This is also what we do when the person has been in the job a long time, but we are a new supervisor. We do this because no matter how good the person seems to be on paper, we don't know yet whether he is going to do the right things. And there is only one definition of "the right things." The right things are the kinds of things we would tell them to do if we had the time and inclination to do so.

So he begins by bringing us recommendations as to how he is going to go about achieving the results for which he is responsible. As we accept these or reject these or ask for modifications of these recommendations, he learns what the right things are. There's no point bringing us recommendations to do "the wrong things," i.e. the kinds of things that he may personally think are swell but at whose mere mention we shudder in horror. There's no point because he is the one responsible for achieving the results, and if he doesn't bring us a recommendation we can approve, he will keep having to listen to why we don't like his proposed actions and will keep getting sent back for new recommendations. He won't be able to start on fulfilling the responsibilities on which he is measured until he comes up with an acceptable plan.

After he has learned the kinds of recommendations we approve, and after he has proven to us over a period of time that he is capable of seeing the right things to do, we should become more trustful of him and more comfortable about the quality of his performance. When our anxiety about what he might do drops, it is time to increase our effectiveness as managers by giving him more control. We do this by moving him to level two, by telling him he needn't bother us anymore with his plan for achieving his results, but we would like to be kept informed as before.

High Anxiety Means Low Control

At first, our anxiety may be such that our checkpoints may be quite frequent, even as often as once a week, depending on our degree of anxiety. At those meetings, we will get an accounting of the things he has been doing. If we find at these meetings that he has suddenly begun to do "the wrong things," we will put him back at level three, asking for a plan of action. But if, sure enough, he is still doing the kind of things we would have told him to do if we had the time and inclination to do that, then we may eventually be comfortable enough to make the checkpoints less frequent. And eventually, less frequent still.

And finally, maybe, he might get to the point where he can graduate to level one. When a volunteer is at level one, there are no checkpoints at all. There are no checkpoints because you have agreed on the result he is trying to achieve, and there is no use in taking his time away from pursuing that objective by bothering him about what he is doing. There is no use because he has proven, over a long enough period for you to be certain, that the things he does are the kinds of things you would tell him to do if you had the time and inclination to do so. If you are not certain, you would not put him at this level.

In those rare cases when volunteers are at level one, management hears from them only if they are having difficulty achieving their results. Otherwise, management assumes that things are on-target and does not need to be bothered with reports that merely confirm this assumption.

Looking Out the Window

In the unlikely event that you are ever lucky enough to get all your people working at level one on all of their responsibilities, you will be able to spend the time you would otherwise spend in making sure people are doing the right things looking out your window, thinking creative and progressive thoughts, thinking strategically about how to handle the future, seeing where trends are leading and grasping the opportunities they offer. That's why managers' offices have windows, to keep that goal forever in your mind.

Usually, volunteers will operate at different levels of control on different responsibilities. For each result, management should tell the volunteer which level of control he has. The way to determine the level of control is to assess your own personal anxiety that the volunteer will go about achieving the target without mishap. If the anxiety is low, the volunteer's degree of control can be high. But if you are worried about errors, the volunteer gets less control so you can make sure the organization achieves the results it requires.

Checkpoints

It is also important to stress that it is only at level one that checkpoints are not used and that people get there only when we are absolutely certain that such checkpoints are not necessary. At all other levels, including level four, managers should keep track of volunteer progress. Even if you have approved an excellent plan, even if you have told a volunteer precisely what to do, it is better to check periodically to make sure he is making progress toward the target than to wait until the end to be surprised that his performance was different than you expected.

A calendar, on which meetings to review volunteer progress are recorded, is the easiest, cheapest, and one of the most effective of all management controls. Not using it is one of the most common management mistakes. By setting regular progress reports, you gain three important advantages, not the least of which is that it lets people know that you are serious about their achievement of their results.

Progress reports also help avoid crises and the poor quality of last-minute work, particularly on long term projects. This is true because the vast majority of human beings spend their work lives reacting to that which is most urgent. Most people begin the work day by surveying the pile of clutter in front of them and asking "What's due first? What am I going to get in the most trouble for not doing today?" They then devote time to that item. If a volunteer has undertaken a project that will take several months to complete, it will not be urgent for quite some time, and so it is easy to put it off until the due date is excruciatingly near. If the volunteer knows he will have to report his progress weekly, the item will become urgent every week on the day before the progress report is due, and so regular progress is insured.

A third advantage of regular progress reports is that they enable the manager to spot problems with an volunteer's work while there is still a chance for corrective action. If the volunteer has misunderstood our intentions, for example, we can find this out early, before the volunteer has wasted a lot of effort going in the wrong direction. Unless the volunteer is at level one on the control scale, remember this motto: If you want it done right, check progress.

Controlling While Empowering

Use of the control scale enables the manager to keep things under control while simultaneously empowering volunteers. Ineffective managers attempt to keep things under control by telling volunteers what to do or by developing rigid procedures, either of which places the volunteer at level four on the control scale. These managers thus have to try to get their results from volunteers who feel belittled and who feel some sense of resentment or apathy as they go about their jobs.

Traditional managers are in this fix in part because they see only two options, they see only levels one and four on the control scale. They see only a choice between controlling things directly or turning people loose to do their own thing, something which would produce chaos. By using the intervening two levels on the control scale, managers using empowering techniques gain the motivational advantages of giving their volunteers a sense of control of their work while also keeping things under control themselves.

Control and Results

This method of keeping things under control while simultaneously empowering the volunteers works only if they have clear results to achieve. Asking for a recommendation when there are no such clear results turns the authority for self-assignment into a guessing game. In the crisis clinic example given earlier, it would have made no sense to ask Frank for a recommendation in situation one if we did not tell him we wanted him to take responsibility for improving the public image. Once he knows what he is supposed to accomplish, he can make an intelligent recommendation. A volunteer needs responsibility before authority makes sense.

Also, it is easier for the supervisor to give the volunteer more control if the results are clearly defined. To return to the crisis clinic example, if the supervisor and Frank both agree that Frank efforts are to be directed toward getting new funding, we will have less anxiety about what he is out there doing than if his responsibilities are murky. And as our anxiety decreases, Frank gets more authority.

By meeting the volunteer's needs for control while simultaneously keeping things under control themselves, effective managers tap a powerful motivator and direct it toward achieving the right results. At the same time, they are able to turn their attention outward, toward the strategic environment in which the organization finds itself. By giving people control of the "how" of their jobs, they are not swamped in the details of the volunteers' performance. As a consequence, they are not taken by surprise by future events and are able to anticipate and use those events to their advantage.

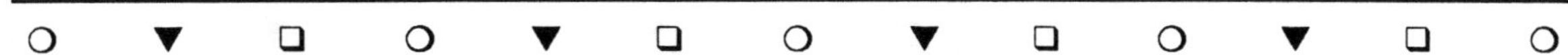

○ ▼ ❑ ○ ▼ ❑ ○ ▼ ❑ ○ ▼ ❑ ○

Chapter Eight

Supervision Systems

Effective Delegation

In addition to the methods of counseling and empowering discussed in the previous chapters, it is also desirable to set up some specific systems to deal with supervisory situations. A variety of these systems will be discussed this chapter.

One of the primary responsibilities of the manager is to delegate responsibility. In a volunteer management system, delegation can occur in a number of formats: volunteer manager to volunteers; agency staff to volunteers; and volunteers to volunteers.

Delegation may often be more difficult in a volunteer relationship because of the separation in time and in geography that is often present. Volunteers may not be 'at the office' except on infrequent occasions, and some volunteers may do most of their work at sites removed from the main worksite. Since this creates a condition in which frequent oversight is more difficult it is critical to be effective at delegation skills.

When delegating tasks to volunteers, the following elements ought to be included in the act of delegation:

1. *Giving the assignment in terms of results:*

   Defining the tasks in terms of what is to be accomplished, not just activities.

2. *Defining the level of control:*

   Informing the volunteer of how much authority they have in making decisions.

3. *Communicating any guidelines:*

   Alerting the volunteer to any parameters which must shape their decisions.

4. *Making resources available:*

   Giving the volunteer the assistance necessary to accomplish the task.

5. *Determining criteria for success:*

   Reaching agreement with the volunteer on how results will be judged.

6. *Setting up checkpoints:*

   Establishing reporting points.

Maintaining Communication

It is also desirable to establish a system for providing on-going supervisory support for the volunteer. There are two main elements necessary for this on-going support:

Availability

Supervisors must be available to the volunteers. The volunteers must have the ability to meet with, report to, and talk with supervisors, both on a regularly scheduled basis and at times of the volunteer's choosing.

This availability will accomplish several things. First, it will directly communicate to the volunteer that their work is appreciated enough to merit the attention and time of the supervisor. Second, it will encourage the volunteer to consult with the supervisor when and if problems are encountered.

Several methods can be instituted to encourage this availability. Open time can be scheduled during the week during which any volunteer can make an appointment. Specific lunch meetings for groups of volunteers can be scheduled during which open discussions are held. Supervisors can practice 'management by walking around' so that they can be approached by volunteers. The intent is to develop a sense of open and ready communication and access.

Equal Status and Involvement

The second key element necessary to on-going supervisory support is a sense among the volunteers that they are being accorded equal status and involvement in agency operations.

This equal treatment includes both participation in decision-making (inclusion in meetings, for example) and participation in day to day activities of the organization (being on memo distribution lists).

The key element in providing a sense of equal status is conveying the impression to the volunteers that they are full partners in activities. This impression can be conveyed (or destroyed) by small differences in treatment (reserved parking for paid staff, with no access by volunteers) to large distinctions (no volunteers are ever invited to attend staff meetings).

A large part of a sense of equal status and involvement can be solved by insuring that volunteers are included in the information flow of the organization. This would inlcude adding them to newsletter mailing lists, making sure they are copied on correspondence that involves their work, or taking the time to update a volunteer who has been absent.

Evaluation and Feedback

It is also important to develop a process for providing evaluation and feedback to the volunteers. While often viewed negatively by those who have to administer it, a good evaluation process is actually of value to those who are judged by it, since it provides them with feedback necessary both to determine how well they are doing and to obtain suggestions on how to improve their perfomance.

In volunteer management, their are two principles to follow in developing an evaluation process:

Regular, Scheduled Feedback

Whatever process that is developed should provide an on-going scheduled evaluation session for each volunteer at a regular interval. The interval should be more frequent when the volunteer first starts (monthly for the first six months) and then should be at least annual.

The benefit of this regular scheduling is that it provides pressure on the supervisor to provide feedback to the volunteer, either through congratulations for work well done or through confronting problems, and it provides reassurance to the volunteer that they will have an opportunity to discuss conditions with their supervisor.

In the absence of regular scheduling, problems tend to be avoided, and instead of being dealt with while minor will develop into major difficulties.

Staff Involvement

Staff members who work with volunteers should be included in the evaluation process. There are two reasons for this involvement. First, if the volunteer is actually being supervised by the staff member, then only the staff member is really in a position to critique the volunteer's work. Second, if the volunteer perceives that the staff person is actually his supervisor, then the volunteer will only be receptive to comments on work from that person, and not from another.

Staff input can be provided either through actual participation in the evaluation session or through input provided to the volunteer manager.

The Positive Side of Evaluation

Rather than thinking of evaluation as a system for dealing with problems, you ought to think about evaluation as a means of rewarding those who are doing well. The percentage of volunteers who are troublesome will be fairly small; those who are hardworking will constitute the vast majority. This means that the majority of evaluation comments can be positive ones, praising the work that is being accomplished.

The evaluation session can also be diagnostic in nature, allowing you to determine how volunteers are feeling about their work. It is quite common, for example, for volunteers who are in intensive job positions (such as providing one-to-one counseling for neglected children) to become 'burned-out'. It is equally common for these volunteers to fail to recognize their problem and to fail to ask for help, since their commitment drives them to continue in their work. The evaluation session can provide the astute volunteer manager with the opportunity to determine whether a good volunteer is becoming burned-out, or bored, or if ready to be promoted to increased responsibility. You may simply determine that the volunteer needs to be rotated to a new job, but you must first have the opportunity to discuss how things are going with the volunteer before you are capapble of knowing what needs to be done. The evaluation session can be turned into a mutual evaluation session with the volunteer, with the intent of rewarding and retaining those who have been productive.

Special Cases

There are two special situations which require particular care in supervision. One involves that of the volunteer who works with little or no connection with the volunteer manager, but is instead 'loaned' or 'assigned' to other staff who are then resopnsible for the volunteer. It is essential to work with those staff until they understand what their responsibilities are in supervising and evaluating the volunteer. Often they will neglect these basic management functions, leaving the volunteer with a feeling of being stranded without any support system.

The second situation involves the 'long distance volunteer', one who works in the field away from day-to-day contact with the organization, and who may perhaps never be physically present in the agency's offices.

It is essential to develp methods of maintaing contact and communication with this volunteer. Consider the use of weekly phone calls to 'check in' and talk with the volunteer, to reduce any feelings of isolation or abandonment.

Firing a Volunteer

Another special situation in which a volunteer manager may find themselves is a decision as to whether or not to terminate the relationship of a volunteer with the agency. The termination might be necessitated either by misconduct (drinking, breach of confidentiality) or unsatisfactory performance (tardiness, inability to complete assignments on a timely basis).

While the decision to fire a volunteer is a perfectly proper one, and, in fact, may be required both in terms of preventing the volunteer from causing additional problems and in terms of maintaining the morale of those with whom the volunteer is working, it is still a serious one. Before making the decision to fire a volunteer, the volunteer manager should first consider if an alternative action is possible.

Alternatives to Firing

There are six alternatives which you might consider:

1. *Re-supervise the volunteer.*
Occasionally you will meet a volunteer who attempts to break rules and simply needs to be reminded that the rules and procedures need to be obeyed. This is very common with teenage volunteers, who will attempt to see what they can get away with during the first month on the job. A firm reminder may be enough to solve the problem.

2. Re-*train the volunteer.*
Some misperformance may be through ignorance. Since many programs operate on the principle of sending a volunteer out to accomplish a task with little training, it is not surprising that some will fail. You may find that the volunteer simply needs are fresher course or needs more extensive training than is common.

3. Re-*motivate the volunteer.*
You may determine that you have a volunteer who is suffering from boredom or a loss of enthusiasm. Attempt to re-interest the volunteer by giving them a new challenge or else consider giving them a sabbatical during which they can refresh their outlook.

4. Re-*assign the volunteer.*
Some disciplinary problems are cases of mismatched personalities. Conflict may have arisen between a volunteer and a staff member, for example, simply because the two do not get along. Neither is inherently bad, but they do not mix or work well together. Rather than punishing the volunteer, consider rematching him with another co-worker, or moving him to a new position for which he is more suitable.

5. Refer *the volunteer to another agency.*
You may be able to address the problem by find a more suitable placement for the volunteer at another agency, where his talents and interests can more productively be utilized.

6. *Retire the volunteer with honor.*

Where you have a volunteer who has given time to the agency for years but has reached a point at which he can no longer contribute, then the appropriate solution may be to arrangement for a retirement party, honoring the contribution which the volunteer has given. You may in fact discover that the volunteer has been wanting to reduce their commitment to the agency, recognizing their own difficulties, but has been deterred from doing so because of a strong sense of obligation to the agency. This formal, but honorable, separation allows the volunteer to leave without guilt.

Establishing a System for Firing

If you do wish to terminate the relationship of a volunteer to the agency, it would be wise to establish a formal system for doing so. The system should:

1. Establish formal policies on probationary service, suspension, and termination, citing the conditions under which a volunteer can be fired or punished.
2. Provide for formal investigation of offenses, with time to learn the volunteer's side of the story and to develop proof of transgression.
3. Have a graduated system of punishment (warning, suspension, termination) and fair and equal enforcement policies.
4. Allow for a review of appeals procedure, including, if you chose, a peer review process.
5. Provide for follow-up notification to staff, clients, and others who need to be informed that the volunteer is no long connected to the agency. It is especially vital to notify any clients with whom the volunteer has been matched that the volunteer is no longer representing or working with the agency.

One side effect of having a system such as this is that it often prompts those who are going through it to make their own determination to leave the agency, thus relieving you of the responsibility for firing them.

○ ▼ ❑ ○ ▼ ❑ ○ ▼ ❑ ○ ▼ ❑ ○

The Firing Interview

The firing of a volunteer should be done personally by the volunteer manager. During the session, follow these principles:

1. *Be quick, direct, and absolute.*

   At some point, make the unequivocal statement that the volunteer is being terminated by the agency.

2. *Announce, don't argue.*

   If you have instituted the firing system described above, you will have already had all necessary discussions and learned all necessary facts. At this point you are handing down the sentence, not re-conducting a trial.

3. *Do not attempt to counsel.*

   If counseling were an alternative you would already have done it. Do not attempt to decieve yourself into believing that they will accept your advice — those whom you have just fired will not regard you as a friend.

4. *Follow up with the volunteer.*

   Confirm the termination in writing in a letter and settle any unfinished logistical items necessary to end the volunteer's relationship with the agency.

While always unpleasant, it is important to be willing to confront a situation which is affecting the agency. Disruptive volunteers, like disruptive paid staff, can stifle the efforts and motivations of those who are attempting to work productively. For the benefit of the good workers, problem volunteers must be dealt with.

Closing

Try to remember two key elements when thinking about your supervisory systems:

- Focus on the positive aspects. Supervision can identify problems when they are small, provide suggestions for improvement, diagnose volunteers who can be helped to do better, and reward achievement.

- Don't feel bad about evaluation. Most people will be winners, and will want to feel like winners, which they can only do if you provide them with feedback. A good part of your motivational job involves giving them that feedback.

○ ▼ ❑ ○ ▼ ❑ ○ ▼ ❑ ○ ▼ ❑ ○

Chapter Nine

Retention and Recognition

Motivation

As has been emphasized throughout this book, volunteer programs are fueled by the motivation of the volunteers and the staff of the agency. Problems of volunteer retention can usually be traced to problems of motivation.

A motivated volunteer is one who wants to do the job that needs to be done in the spirit and within the guidelines desired by the agency. People behave in motivated ways when that behavior meets some need of theirs. Children, for example, are motivated to open birthday presents because doing so meets a psychological need. Starting here, we correctly see that volunteer motivation comes from inside the volunteer, stemming from a set of needs which are satisfied by doing things which are found to be productive.

When we encounter a volunteer who is not behaving as we would like, we tend to label them 'unmotivated', but actually this is incorrect. A so-called unmotivated person is just as motivated as a 'motivated' person is. He too needs, wants, and desires something. However, for reasons we will explore in this chapter, those needs are not seen to be met by behaving in the 'proper' ways. But the behavior which is being chosen does satisfy them more than the behavior we would like them to choose.

All Behavior is Motivated

Sometimes, "unmotivated" behavior is caused by the frustration of a motivational need. If a volunteer has a high need for achievement, for example, and he doesn't see that what he does in his volunteer experience is meeting that need, he may chose to set up a win-lose situation with those in authority. In one volunteer fire department, for example, a volunteer would go to the board of commissioners every time the Chief disagreed with him, seeking to get the Chief's decision overturned. This so called "unmotivated" behavior met the volunteer's need for achievement; it gave him something to try to win.

When we talk about motivating volunteers, therefore, we aren't talking about changing what is inside an individual. We aren't talking about creating new needs. What we are talking about is creating a volunteer experience which allows an individual to meet his or her motivational needs in ways that are productive for the organization and satisfying for the individual. We make sure, in other words, that a volunteer receives his "motivational paycheck" for the valuable contributions he makes to our agency. This is the essence of volunteer retention.

Setting up conditions that meet the motivational needs of volunteers is a complicated and challenging task because each volunteer brings a different combination of needs to the job. It is further complicated because a volunteer's needs may change as the conditions in the rest of his life change. The following are the major motivational needs most volunteers bring, in some combination, to the job today.

Basic Motivational Needs

The Need for Recognition

This is the need people have to be held in esteem by others. This may take the form of appreciation for their work or the form of approval for the qualities they exhibit. This will be discussed later in this chapter.

The Need for Achievement

This is the need people have to feel they are accomplishing something. This need is met by people who have some clear goal in mind that they are working toward. If jobs are designed according to the principles presented in Chapter Two, this need will be met.

The Need for Control

This is the need people have to feel that they are independent, that they are in charge of their lives. It is met when people make their own decisions about the actions that they take. If volunteers are supervised according to the principles described in the previous chapter on empowering volunteers, this need will be met.

The Need for Variety

Human beings tend to get bored "doing the same old thing." Volunteering itself helps meet people's need for variety in life. At the same time, however, we must be on the lookout for volunteers getting tired of the job they do and offer to increase, expand, or change their duties from time to time so that they have fresh challenges in their lives.

The Need for Growth

This is the need people have to feel that they are developing, that they are increasing their skills, knowledge, or status in life. This need is met in volunteer programs through the training, coaching, and counseling techniques described earlier.

The Need for Affiliation

This is the need people have to belong, to share, to be accepted, to be loved, to cooperate, and to be connected with another person or group. This need will be explored more fully in this chapter.

The Need for Power

This is the need people have to be able to influence the actions of others. It is met by exercising positions of leadership, by rising to higher positions in organizations, and by persuading others to do what the individual wants. Volunteers motivated by this need "get paid" by fulfilling positions of influence in an organization, such as being a board member, a spokesperson, or a coordinator of a project.

The Need for Fun

Although this may seem frivolous, the need for fun and adventure is a very strong need, sometimes outweighing all others. It is met when people are engaged in activities they find exciting or enjoyable.

The Need for Uniqueness

This is the need to feel special. It is a major component of self-esteem, granting the volunteer a sense of individual worth. This need will be explored more later.

To Each His Own Mix

Not all volunteers are motivated by all of these needs. Some volunteers may care little about power or achievement, for example, and care a lot about affiliation. Others may be just the opposite. Also, a volunteer's needs may change over time. A volunteer may be quite happy doing a job that requires a great deal of independent action, for example, but on getting a divorce suddenly have a great need for affiliation. In such a circumstance, the volunteer director might continue the person's motivational paycheck by changing the job to one that is done in a group setting.

The art of motivating volunteers lies not only in knowing how to tap a given motivator, but in being able to figure out what combination of the above needs a particular volunteer brings to the job. One way to do that is to ask the volunteers periodically. Discuss with the volunteer their rating of the relative importance of the following in terms of their own satisfaction:

- Gain knowledge of community problems.
- Maintain skills no longer used otherwise.
- Spend time with members of the family by volunteering together.
- Get out of the house.
- Make new friends.
- Be with old friends who volunteer here.
- Gain new skills.
- Have fun.
- Meet a challenge.
- Improve my community.
- Work with a certain client group.
- Be in charge of something.

- Be part of a group or a team.
- Get experience to get a job.
- Meet important people in the community.
- Gain status with my employer.
- Get community recognition.

The mix of responses by the volunteer will give you a better feeling for why they decided to volunteer and what you need to attempt to give them in return as their 'motivational paycheck'.

Retention

The key to retention is to make sure the volunteers are getting their particular complex of motivational needs met through the volunteer experience. When this is occurring on a large scale, a positive, enthusiastic climate is created which, in turn, encourages people to continue to volunteer.

When we set about creating such a motivating environment, there are two needs which most people have that deserve special attention. Those motivational needs are th*e need to feel a sense of belonging* and *the need for autonomy*. These may seem like contradictory aspects, and in most people's lives they are. We have all known environments in which one or the other aspect is apparent but seldom do we see both together.

The needs for belonging and uniqueness are basic human motivational needs. Many of us spend our lives compromising between the two, giving up some of our uniqueness in order to gain a feeling of belonging, or giving up some of our connectedness in order to become more autonomous, more powerful, more a separate and unique person. Most of us have had experiences in which we were being smothered by our need to belong and yearned to be more autonomous, to be able to make our own decisions about our lives. And most of us have also had experiences in which we yearned for a feeling of connectedness. It is rare that both of these needs are satisfied simultaneously. If we can create an environment in which people simultaneously feel part of a group and unique, we unleash tremendous motivational power and a tremendous desire to volunteer at our agency.

Meeting the Need for Belonging

There are several aspects of creating such a climate. To meet the needs for belonging or connectedness, we can do such things as:

- Establish mutual goals.
- Recruit volunteers with similar interests.
- Recruit volunteers with similar values.
- Through empowering, establish a climate of trust.
- Give recognition to the team of volunteers as a group.

Meeting the Need for Autonomy

To meet the needs for autonomy and uniqueness, we can do such things as:

- Give volunteers more authority.
- Seek volunteer opinions.
- Define their jobs in terms of results.
- Treat volunteers as important contributors to the organization.
- Provide feedback on individual performance.
- Measure individual performance in achieving results.

One way in which we can meet both needs simultaneously is by seeking and implementing the suggestions of volunteers. This is critical not only to the creation of a positive climate but to the effectiveness of an organization. In this fast-changing world, we cannot afford to do tomorrow that which we did yesterday. The organization must change, grow, evolve. This means that it must constantly think about better ways of doing things. Volunteers are an important source of these innovative ideas.

Promoting Innovation

Innovative ideas do not have to be major, earth-shattering changes. Rather it is the cumulative effect of thousands of small changes that enables us to continue to meet the challenge of remaining effective in an ever changing world. One of the reasons that Japanese companies have been so successful is that they implement hundreds of thousands of worker ideas for small improvements every year. In 1987, Toyota implemented over one million such suggestions. We can encourage such behavior in our volunteers by actively seeking their opinions, asking questions such as:

What are some better ways of doing what we do?

If you were in charge here, what would you change?

We can also occasionally ask the group to get involved in brainstorming such ideas, asking questions such as:

If we were to go across the street and start a competing organization, what would we do differently over there? How could we do a better job of serving our clients?

Asking for ideas is not enough by itself, however. If none of these ideas are ever implemented, people will get discouraged and stop making suggestions. If the ideas you receive are not good enough to implement or would actually make things worse, or if they are somehow in conflict with the values or goals of the larger organization, you should tell the volunteer your concerns and ask him to modify the idea so that it does not have those drawbacks.

When people feel that their ideas are sought and implemented, they feel unique and powerful. At the same time, however, they feel a greater sense of identification with the organization, because they had a hand in shaping it. They feel valued as individuals and they feel connected to the whole. By thereby creating an environment in which volunteers feel both connected and unique, we create a loyalty and a desire to continue to volunteer.

Recognition

As noted above, volunteers must also receive a sense of appreciation and reward for their contribution. This sense can be conveyed through a number of processes, including both formal and informal recognition systems.

Formal Recognition Systems

Formal recognition systems comprise the awards, certificates, plaques, pins, and recognition dinners held or presented in honor of volunteer achievement. Many volunteer organizations hold an annual ceremony in which individual volunteers are singled out for achievement. The event is often held during National Volunteer Week to coincide with a community celebration of volunteer achievement.

In determining whether or not to establish such a formal ceremony, consider the following:

- ✓ Is this being done to honor the volunteer or so that staff can feel involved and can feel that they have shown their appreciation for volunteers?
- ✓ Is it real, and not stale or pro forma?
- ✓ Does it fit? Would the volunteers feel better if we spent the money on the clients instead of on a rubber chicken luncheon?
- ✓ Can we make it a sense of celebration and a builder of group identity?

While formal recognition systems are a useful tool, they cannot substitute for on-going processes which meet the motivational needs of the volunteer. They are helpful mainly in satisfying the needs of the volunteer who has a need for community approval, but have little impact (and occasionally have a negative impact) on volunteers whose primary focus is helping the clientele. Those volunteers may very well feel more motivated and recognized by a system which recognizes the achievements of 'their' clients, and also recognizes the contribution which the volunteer has made in aiding in that achievement.

Informal Recognition

The most effective recognition system occurs in the day-to-day interchange between the volunteer and the agency through the sincere appreciation and thanks of the staff for the work being done by the volunteer.

This type of recognition is more effective in part because it is much more frequent; a dinner once a year does not carry the same impact as 365 days of good working relationships.

Day-to-day recognition may include such items as:

- Saying 'thank you'.
- Involving the volunteer in decisions that affect them.
- Asking about the volunteer's family and showing an interest.

- Making sure that volunteers receive equal treatment to that of staff.
- Sending a note of appreciation to a volunteer's family.
- Allowing the volunteer to attend community training events.
- Recommending the volunteer for promotion.
- Remembering the volunteer's birthday.
- Celebrating the volunteer's anniversary date with the agency.

The intent of day-to-day recognition is to convey a constant sense of appreciation and belonging to the volunteer. This sense can be better conveyed by the thousands of small interactions that compose daily life than it can be conveyed in an annual ceremonial event.

Rules for Recognition

Whatever mix of recognition system you utilize, remember the following rules:

1. *Give it or else.*

   If volunteers don't get the recognition they want from you, they will get it from someone else, and not necessarily for the behavior you wish to encourage.

2. *Give it frequently.*

   People want to be recognized. Give recognition and praise frequently to enhance people's image of themselves as 'winners.'

3. *Public forum, peer group.*

   Recognition is most effective when given publicly, and is even more effective when it is bestowed in the presence of a peer group. An example of this is praising the work of a volunteer during a staff meeting.

4. *Time it properly.*

   Recognition is enhanced by a closeness to the behavior which is being praised. An award eight months after an accomplishment does not have the same impact as a simple 'good job' at the immediate completion of a task.

5. *Target the recognition method*

   Try to match the method of recognition to the individual. A person who is volunteering to enhance their career, for example, might best feel recognized through a letter from the chairman of the agency board to their employer, praising the accomplishments of the volunteer.

6. *Be consistent and sincere.*

   Do not recognize false achievement and do not recognize some people and not others for the same levels of achievement. If people believe that your recognition is arbitrary or unrelated to accomplishment they will not believe it even when it is given to the right people.

7. *Recognize achievement, but praise the person.*

   Recognition is most effective when it is given for a specific achievement (such as completing a project), but it is even more effective when the phrasing of the recognition is directed at the individual, not just the accomplishment: "I can always count on you to do a great job and get it done on time." Think of phrasing your praise in terms of "You have done a good job" and not "This is a good job."

Closing

Retention and recognition might best be thought of as 'small is beautiful' activities. They are both better accomplished when related to the specific individual, not the entire program of volunteers, and they are best done in day-to-day increments rather than a single massive event. This does not mean that events and ceremonial awards do not have their place (especially in volunteer situations with a high sense of group identity), but it does mean that you should never imagine that the occasional formal praise can ever take the place of what happens on a daily basis in informal interactions.

Chapter Ten

Volunteer-Staff Relations

The Eternal Triangle

Many new volunteer managers make the mistake of believing that the major item to work on in the program is the relationship between themselves and 'their' volunteers. They envision the work as developing a better straight line continuum:

Envisioning the job in this way is actually quite dangerous. The true working arrangement in most programs is more like a 3-way arrangement, a triangle, than it is a 2-way arrangement:

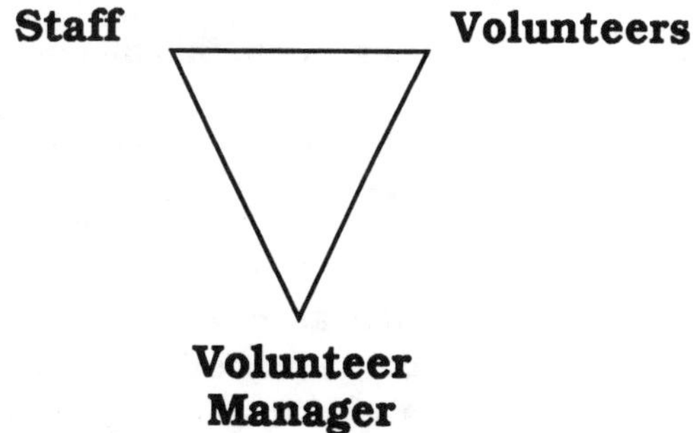

The triangle arrangement is present whenever volunteers will be working with paid staff in the agency, either directly assigned to them or else assisting in their departments, projects, or with their clients. If any of these conditions are true, then it is necessary to think of the working relationship as concerning three groups, and it is necessary for the volunteer manager to devote an equal portion of time to establishing good relationships with staff.

Dealing with Staff Concerns

A good volunteer manager will begin by recognizing that staff may have legitimate fears or concerns about the utilization of volunteers.

The concerns may be organizational in nature:

- a fear of loss of control
- a fear of diminished quality of service
- a fear that volunteers will be unreliable
- a fear of increased legal problems.

The concerns may be personal in nature:

- a resentment of increased work load
- a fear of loss of a job
- a fear of having to manage volunteers when staff have no experience.

The role of the volunteer manager is to determine the concerns of the staff and then turn these concerns into a sense of confidence among the staff that the volunteers will be a useful addition to the agency.

In general, this means imparting two feelings to staff:

A sense of benefit greater than the difficulties
A feeling of control

Staff are more likely to be 'satisfied' with the volunteer program if they can perceive that the return to them is greater than the effort involved, and if they can perceive that they are highly involved in making decisions that affect their degree of involvement with volunteers.

In dealing with staff concerns, it is wise to note that your natural instincts (to 'fight and win') may be disastrous. Many volunteer managers attempt to deal with staff concerns by utilizing power, often through seeking a top management mandate that 'volunteers **will** be assigned to all staff.'

This approach is fatal. It will leave the staff seeking revenge for what has been imposed upon them and they will exercise this revenge upon the only available target—the volunteers.

Such a situation is also likely to involve you in unpleasant political games. These affect the organizational climate in adverse ways. In cases where there is lot of conflict among staff, where there is a 'war zone' atmosphere, volunteer turnover will be higher than otherwise. If a volunteer senses a lot of tension and conflict in the organization, they will be deterred from continuing to work. Volunteer time is discretionary time, and most people would prefer to spend their discretionary time in a pleasant environment.

Another fatal approach is the use of criticism. Arguing with staff is futile; telling them five reasons why they are wrong is futile. Many of the concerns of staff will not be built entirely on logic, and, indeed, may not even be directly related to the volunteer program. Directly confronting staff may only produce a defensiveness that will turn to hostility if you continue to push the issue.

The correct way to deal with staff concerns is through acting as a consultant to staff, seeking to assist them via counseling into recognizing why the utilization of volunteers would be appropriate for them.

Consulting with Staff

In order to be effective with staff, we need to take a different approach, an approach which we call the Consulting Method. This approach has a lot in common with the counseling techniques discussed earlier in that it relies on the use of questions to empower staff to discover action that will help them. The role of the volunteer manager in this case is one of assisting staff in finding ways to make their work easier.

An Example of Consulting

Imagine that you are talking to a staff member about involving volunteers and he says that he doesn't want to take the time to do it. The natural instinct at this point might be to tell him how wrong he is to have this attitude or to tell him that agency policy requires volunteer use. The consulting approach, however, asks questions instead, as the following conversation illustrates:

"Do you mean you don't see the value of having volunteers working here?"

"Well, it sounds good in theory. But they aren't reliable. You spend a lot of time training them, and then they don't show up."

Again, your natural instinct at this point might be to say "They would if you treated them better." Instead, biting your lip, you say "Why do you suppose that is?"

"What do you mean?"

"Why don't they show up?"

"I don't know. I guess they probably have other things to do."

"Why would they prefer those other things?"

"I don't know. I guess they're probably more fun."

"Is there any way we could make this job more fun."

"I don't think so, it's a pretty boring job."

"Why is that? What makes it so boring?"

"Well, it's pretty repetitive."

"Could we redesign the job to make it less repetitive and more interesting?"

"That sounds like a lot of work."

"That's what you have me for."

The Consultant as Helper

At this point you are offering yourself as a resource to help the staff person. If he says something like "What could you do?", he is in effect asking if you could help him solve a problem. This is a very different relationship than one in which you are trying to make him use volunteers. In this instance, if he does ask for help, you could work with the staff person, using the principles of motivating job design described in Chapter Three.

Building Staff Support

There are a number of steps you will want to add to this consulting approach in order to gain staff support for the volunteer program. The steps and suggestions are designed to both deal with staff fears and concerns and to assist staff as they attempt to make use of volunteers. We have divided the suggestions into things to do before placement of volunteers, while staff are attempt to deal with volunteers, and after volunteers have been in place for a time.

Before Placement of Volunteers

Before any staff have been assigned volunteers, it is helpful to have done the following:

- *Develop an Agency Policy on Volunteer Involvement*

  This policy should be adopted and supported by top policy makers, and it should be integrated into the overall agency plan for activity and growth. It should be taken into account when determining staff workloads. While the policy should be adopted, it should not be phrased as a mandate, and there should be no attempt to require that all staff must utilize volunteers.

- *Background Research*

  As mentioned in Chapter Two, a survey or assessment process should ascertain staff experience levels in working with volunteers, staff fears and concerns, and staff needs for additional training or materials. You should also continue this research process while staff are beginning to utilize volunteers, perhaps through the scheduling of a monthly meeting at which staff can discuss their needs or even through the creation of a 'volunteer users group'.

- *Job Development Process*

  The volunteer manager should work individually with each department and each staff person to assist them in development of good volunteer jobs. Follow the suggestions in Chapter Three for how to carry out this process.

- *Staff Utilization Plan*

  Assist each staff person in developing a plan for how they will utilize volunteers. Include such items as "Where will the volunteer be working", "What equipment will the volunteer need", "Who will be in charge of the volunteer," "Where will new assignments come from".

- *Staff Orientation and Training*

  Staff should receive an orientation and training session on effective management of volunteers. They should understand who will be volunteering for the agency and what the volunteers will want in return for their involvement. In effect, you should train your staff to be volunteer supervisors.

During Placement of Volunteers

While volunteers are being matched with staff, you should consider the following:

- *Involve Staff in Screening, Interviewing, and Training*

  Those staff who are afraid of a loss of quality control will be made more comfortable if they are included in the selection and preparation process. Allow them to help develop the criteria by which volunteers will be chosen, to participate in interviewing potential volunteers for their department, and to design and present portions of the volunteer training sessions.

- *Clarification of Roles and Responsibilities*

  Be sure that you clarify the web of relationships between the volunteer, the staff person and the volunteer manager. The staff person must understand whether supervision is being done by themselves or by the volunteer manager. Staff must understand who is in charge of what, who is responsible for what, and what should happen if things go wrong. Who, for example, is in charge of firing an unsatisfactory volunteer? The staff person? The volunteer manager? Is it a unilateral decision or a joint one?

- *Monitor After Placement*

  Do not assume that all first matchings of a staff member and a volunteer will succeed. It is wise to conduct frequent check-ups during the period after placement to ensure that a good fit has been attained. Check for verification of skills and qualifications adequate to do the job, amity between the staff and volunteer, and general staff comfort with their ability to work with the volunteer.

- *Staff Involvement in Management*

  Continue to include the staff person in management and supervision of the volunteer. The extent of this involvement may vary from staff person to staff person, depending upon their own comfort and desire for management responsibilities. Even if the volunteer manager still 'controls' and supervises the volunteer, an effort should be made to make the staff person feel a part of the supervisory team and to keep them informed about what is happening. You can do this by 'asking their advice' from time to time about how the volunteer should be treated, or inquiring as to how they think the volunteer is doing at the job.

After Placement of Volunteers

To encourage increased use of volunteers after they have initially been placed, consider doing the following:

- *Provide Feedback on Results*

  Develop evaluation results that can be provided to staff showing the effectiveness of utilizing volunteers. These results could range from a report on the volunteer hours being contributed to their departments to simple stories and testimonials praising volunteer activity.

- *Develop New Ideas on Volunteer Use*

  Continue to assist staff in developing new things that volunteers can do. Circulate examples of creative volunteer utilization. Remember that some of your staff will be very supportive of volunteers, and you must provide assistance to these 'high end users' as well as support to those who are having difficulties.

- *Reward Staff who are Doing A Good Job*

  The reward system may include the creation of a formal award for staff who have best utilized volunteer resources. It may include arranging for top management praise. It is essential, however, that recognition be provided to those who are working effectively with volunteers, both to motivate their work and to encourage others to emulate their example.

Creating Senior Management Support

A special situation related to staff support for the volunteer program is that relating to the involvement of senior management, who must not only endorse the use of volunteers by staff but must also endorse and support the concept of a volunteer program. We will now discuss the ways in which the volunteer program can gain the support of the upper staff levels.

Keys to Management Support

There are three elements which are essential in gaining support from senior management:

- *Understanding*

  Senior management staff must understand the volunteer program in terms of what it does and how it operates, including the relationship that the volunteer program needs to have with other staff.

- *Information*

  Senior management staff must understand what the volunteer program can accomplish compared to the financial and personnel costs required to operate the program, and must understand that the benefits gained outweigh the costs.

- *Involvement*

  Senior management staff must understand what they can and should do to assist the program, and how they should be involved with other staff and with volunteers.

Understanding

Obtaining a firm commitment by senior management requires first that they actually understand the nature of the volunteer program.

This requires first that they themselves know why they wish to have volunteers connected with the agency. Senior management must be secure in their decision to support a volunteer program, and that security should rest in their own belief that the volunteers have the ability to contribute to the success of the agency.

Their decision should be based on whatever rationale they choose to adopt, whether viewing volunteers as a source of community input or community outreach, or simply viewing volunteers as a means of cost-effective service delivery. The particular rationale is not as important as the fact that **some** commonly accepted rationale must be in place. If there is not one in your agency it would be wise to lead senior staff through a planning exercise to formulate one. If you do not do this you risk having several different, and perhaps mutually exclusive, opinions of why the volunteer program should exist, or risk the possibility that no one in senior management really understands why it does exist. It is difficult to fully support that which you do not fully understand.

Tied to this rationale is a second requirement, that senior management understand what needs to be done in order to have an effective volunteer program. They must have an overview of the volunteer management process and an understanding of the investment the agency needs to make in order to effectively make use of volunteers. This should include a clear understanding of the requirements in terms of staff time, money, sharing power, etc, that will be necessary in order to achieve a fully-functioning volunteer program.

Information

The second element necessary to management support is sufficient information to judge whether the program is successful.

This information can take a number of forms.

Volunteer Utilization Patterns

It might consist of reports of where and how volunteer are being utilized. A report would include, for example, a department-by-department listing of how many volunteers are involved, how many hours they are contributing, and what types of jobs they are doing. The value of this type of report is that it allows senior management to identify patterns of usage, highlighting staff and departments who are doing a good job of involving volunteers and those who are not.

It also shows senior management the types of work that volunteers are capable of doing for the agency.

Value of Volunteer Utilization

It is also valuable to include estimates of what the value to the agency is of the volunteer contribution. This would include tracking a number of items:

- *Value of Donated Volunteer Time:*
  computing the number of volunteer hours and multiplying it by an estimated hourly wage.

- *In-Kind Donations:*
  recording the value of any in-kind contributions obtained by volunteers in their work, including use of their own personal equipment or items they obtain from their paid jobs.

- *Un-reimbursed Volunteer Expenses:*
  tracking the expenses incurred by volunteers (mileage, phone calls, copying) for which they do not require agency reimbursement.

Information should be provided to senior management in a combination of facts (statistics, lists, etc) and stories (anecdotes, examples, interesting volunteers).

Involvement

The final element in senior management support involves telling them how and when to be helpful to the program.

There are several functions at which an appearance by senior management is extremely valuable. These include appearing at volunteer orientations, giving out volunteer recognition items, meeting occasionally with groups of volunteers. It also includes being supportive on an on-going basis of the volunteer program. One excellent example of top management support occurs in a hospital whose chief administrator has an hourly meeting with volunteers each Tuesday, rotating the invitees among different departments.

Senior managers also need instruction on how to assist in encouraging other staff. The most difficult point to get across may be to remind them that you are not interested in having them coerce staff into utilizing volunteers. Work with them on ways to reward staff who work well with volunteers, and allow the absence of reward to convince other staff that they should work harder.

Closing

Follow these three general principles in planning your work with staff:

- Try to spend at least as much time working with staff as you do working directly with the volunteers. In the initial development of your program plan to spend much more time with the staff.

- Deal with problems that arise as quickly as possible. Do not let a situation fester. And do not attempt to force people to get along. It is better for the volunteer to be transferred elsewhere than for you to try to enforce compatibility.

- Your ultimate objective is to get the staff to do the core work of volunteer management. If you can enable staff to become effective volunteer managers then you will be able to spend your time working on creative job development and troubleshooting. If you are forced to attempt to supervise all of the volunteers in the agency then you will be overwhelmed by the trivial.

Chapter Eleven

Some Final Suggestions

Finding an Overall Approach

In tackling the work outlined in the previous chapters it is essential to employ a coherent philosophical approach. Our suggestion for this approach would have you concentrate on two theories, which we think will make success more probable.

Start small, and grow with success.

Do not expect to accomplish everything at once and do not try to. Operating a volunteer program is a delicate and complicated task, made so in part by the fact that the more successful you are at some things (such as recruitment), then the more work you will create for yourself. It is better to begin with little things and grow a bit at a time than to become over-extended and create bad feelings with unsuccessful volunteer placements. Happy staff and happy volunteers will become your best salespeople for the program, but you have to make sure that they are happy.

Rely on persuasion, not coercion.

Do not try to force volunteers on the agency or on any staff person. The utilization of volunteers will help an agency, but only if the agency chooses to allow it. Rely on the persuasion of competence and success—if staff see that some departments are gaining benefits through the use of volunteers then eventually they will decide to gain the same advantages for themselves. Have confidence in the value of your resource, and be willing to let people come to you rather than feeling compelled to beg them. Never be foolish enough to believe that you can coerce anyone into utilizing volunteers. A good, small volunteer program is much more valuable than an ineffective large one.

The Geometry of Volunteer Involvement

As you think about operating the program, try to keep in mind the simple geometric shapes:

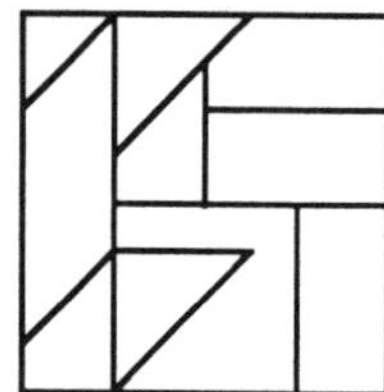

The Puzzle Square
representing the jobs which the agency needs done.

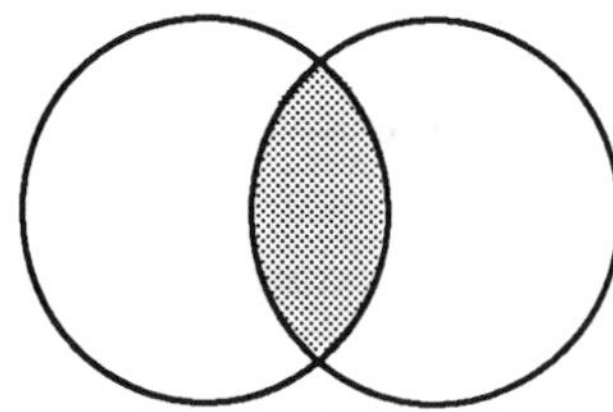

The Overlapping Circles
representing the commonly met needs of the agency and the volunteers.

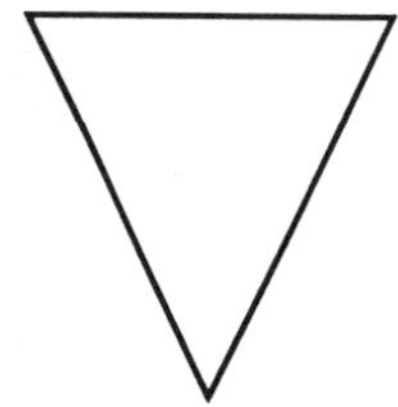

The Triangle
representing the web of relationships among the volunteer manager, the volunteer, and staff.

If you can construct a program which embodies these three shapes, you will have created a program which will effectively utilize volunteer resources.

Getting Help

There are a variety of places where you can obtain help in learning more about volunteer management. These include:

- National organizations such as:

  VOLUNTEER: The National Center;
  the Association for Volunteer Administration;
  the National Association of Partners in Education; and
  the American Society of Directors of Volunteer Service.

- State groups, including Governors office of volunteer services.

- Local groups of volunteer administrators, sometimes called DOVIAs.

You will also discover that your greatest need for help will be in obtaining additional personnel to aid you in performing the labor intensive part of volunteer management. In fact, the better you are at recruiting and involving volunteers, then the more planning and interpersonal contact that will become necessary within your program.

The best remedy for this dilemma is to begin to recruit volunteers to assist you in volunteer adminstration. This not only presents a consistent image to other staff (who otherwise would say, "If you don't use volunteers, then why should I?"), but will also give you the support to spend time on the more skilled portions of your work. Especially look for volunteers who can help you in interviewing and recruiting.

The Golden Rule

Finally, remember the Golden Rule of Volunteer Management:

"Their niceness will let you recruit a volunteer the first time, but only your competence will let you keep them..."

Bibliography

Susan Ellis

- *From the Top Down* (Philadelphia: Energize Associates) 1986.

Susan Ellis and Katherine Noyes

- *By the People: A History of Americans as Volunteers* (Philadelphia: Energize Associates) 1978.
- *No Excuses: The Team Approach to Volunteer Management* (Philadelphia: Energize Associates) 1981.
- *Proof Positive: Developing Significant Volunteer Recordkeeping Systems* (Philadelphia: Energize Associates) 1980.

Kathleen Brown Fletcher

- *The Nine Keys to Successful Volunteer Programs* (Washington: Taft Group) 1987.

Rick Lynch

- *Developing Your Leadership Potential* (Downers Grove: VMSystems) 1988.
- *Precision Management* (Seattle: Abbott Press) 1986.

Marilyn MacKenzie

- *Dealing with Difficult Volunteers* (Downers Grove: VMSystems) 1988.

Steve McCurley

- *Volunteer Management Forms* (Downers Grove: VMSystems) 1988.

Steve McCurley and Sue Vineyard

- *101 Ideas for Volunteer Programs* (Downers Grove: VMSystems) 1986.
- *101 Tips for Volunteer Recruitment* (Downers Grove: VMSystems) 1988.

Ivan Scheier

- *Winning with Staff* (Boulder: NICOV) 1978.

Nora Silver

- *At the Heart: The New Volunteer Challenge to Community Agencies* (Pleasanton: Valley Volunteer Center) 1988.

Sue Vineyard

- *Beyond Banquets, Plaques, and Pins: Creative Ways to Recognize Volunteers* (Downers Grove: VMSystems) 1989.
- *Evaluating Volunteers, Programs, and Events* (Downers Grove: VMSystems) 1988.

Marlene Wilson

- *The Effective Management of Volunteer Programs* (Boulder: Volunteer Management Associates) 1976.